Corporate Strategy and Financial Decisions

Corporate Strategy and Financial Decisions

Tony Grundy

KOGAN
PAGE

First published in 1992

Kogan Page Ltd
120 Pentonville Road
London N1 9JN

© Tony Grundy 1992

British Library Cataloguing in Publication Data
A CIP record of this book is available from the British Library.

ISBN 0 7494 0774 1

Typeset by Books Unlimited (Nottm) – Sutton-in-Ashfield, Notts. NG17 1AL
Printed and bound in Great Britain by Biddles Ltd, Guildford and Kings Lynn

CONTENTS

LIST OF FIGURES

LIST OF TABLES

THE CRANFIELD MANAGEMENT RESEARCH SERIES

The Cranfield Management Research Series represents an exciting joint initiative between the Cranfield School of Management and Kogan Page.

As one of Europe's leading post-graduate business schools, Cranfield is renowned for its applied research activities, which cover a wide range of issues relating to the practice of management.

Each title in the Series is based on current research and authored by Cranfield faculty or their associates. Many of the research projects have been undertaken with the sponsorship and active assistance of organisations from the industrial, commercial or public sectors. The aim of the Series is to make the findings of direct relevance to managers through texts which are academically sound, accessible and practical.

For managers and academics alike, the Cranfield Management Research Series will provide access to up-to-date management thinking from some of Europe's leading academics and practitioners. The series represents both Cranfield's and Kogan Page's commitment to furthering the improvement of management practice in all types of organisations.

THE SERIES EDITORS

Frank Fishwick
Reader in Managerial Economics
Director of Admissions at Cranfield School of Management

Frank joined Cranfield from Aston University in 1966, having previously worked in textiles, electronics and local government (town and country planning). Recent research and consultancy interests have been focused on business concentration, competition policy and the book publishing industry. He has been directing a series of research studies for the

Commission of the European Communities, working in collaboration with business economists in France and Germany. Frank is permanent economic adviser to the Publishers Association in the UK and is a regular consultant to other public and private sector organisations in the UK, continental Europe and the US.

Gerry Johnson
Professor of Strategic Management
Director of the Centre for Strategic Management and Organisational Change
Director of Research at Cranfield School of Management

After graduating from University College London, Gerry worked for several years in management positions in Unilever and Reed International before becoming a Management Consultant. Since 1976, he has taught at Aston University Management Centre, Management Business School, and from 1988 at Cranfield School of Management. His research work is primarily concerned with processes of strategic decision making and strategic change in organisations. He also works as a consultant on issues of strategy formulation change at a senior level with a number of UK and international firms.

Shaun Tyson
Professor of Human Resource Management
Director of the Human Resource Research Centre
Dean of the Faculty of Management and Administration at Cranfield School of Management

Shaun studied at London University and spent eleven years in senior positions in industry within engineering and electronic companies.

For four years he was a lecturer in personnel management at the Civil Service College, and joined Cranfield in 1979. He has acted as a consultant and researched widely into human resource strategies, policies and the evaluation of the function. He has published eight books.

PREFACE

The idea for researching the linkages between corporate strategy and
financial decisions came to me when I was planning, finance and
acquisitions manager of an international company during 1987.

I had previously written a booklet extolling the virtues of prescriptive
techniques of evaluating investment decisions for one of the accounting
bodies. However, when I became involved at the cutting edge of
appraising acquisition opportunities, R&D and other organic investment,
these prescriptions seemed naive and over-simplified. I then began a long
journey of research at Cranfield to explore how corporate strategy and
longer-term financial decisions can be linked in major organisations. This
book now contains the insights of this work in a form designed to be of
practical relevance. Accordingly, details of research methodology have
been placed in Appendix 2 for the more academic reader.

The ideas and frameworks put forward in this book are not put forward
in support of any 'management fashion' – they are based on empirical
study and the frameworks presented aim at being practical and
implementable. The practising manager will find the checklists in
Appendix 1 particularly helpful: these have been based not only on the
research but also on lessons from my advisory work with major
companies.

ACKNOWLEDGEMENTS

I would like to thank a number of key players in this study. First, I am indebted to Professor Gerry Johnson who endured my endless enthusiasm for this task and who pointed me away from prescriptive thinking. I would also like to thank all eight participants in the research who invested their valuable time in co-exploring their issues with me. These included Simon Hart and Austin Brackin of Rolls Royce; David Shephard and Doug Waddell of IDV (part of Grand Met); John Vaughan and Peter Clark of London Underground Limited; and David Marshall and Andy Cook at Post Office Counters Limited. Also, it was invaluable to have the support and involvement of my past colleagues at KPMG Peat Marwick including David Bishop and Mike Bottomley. I am grateful, too, to Simon Woolley of BP who helped me on value-based management, to CIMA and to John Constable who reviewed the book prior to publication. Not least, I would also thank my team of word-processing experts who churned through over two thousand pages of my word-for-word transcriptions, my Doctoral thesis and this book itself.

The initial funding for the research was kindly provided by a research fellowship of the Institute of Chartered Accountants in England and Wales.

PART ONE - PROBLEMS AND TOOLS

INTRODUCTION

This book gives managers both a practical and theoretical guide on how to link strategic and financial appraisal at corporate and business levels and at the level of major strategic projects. It focuses on how, by linking strategic and financial appraisal, greater vision can be injected into the *value* appraisal process of decisions which are not only strategic but also are financial. This is applicable to developing new business strategies, reviewing existing businesses within the corporate portfolio or when making major investment decisions. The book therefore covers a range of topics rarely touched on in one source – both strategy and value and at a number of levels within a corporate body and the process of making major organic or acquisitive corporate financial decisions. Our ambitious task is facilitated with the use of case material on five large organisations – Rolls Royce, Grand Met (IDV), London Underground, Post Office Counters, and finally, BP. These research cases are also enriched by selected input from the author's past line management and consultancy experience, particularly in Chapters 1, 2 and 5.

WHAT IS THE PROBLEM AND WHY DOES IT EXIST?

First, it is necessary to 'define the problem' which is at the root of difficulties in linking strategic and financial appraisal. The practising manager should be quick to recognise these symptoms. This may be best done by contrasting the approaches of strategic and financial appraisal, as shown in Table 1.1

Table 1.1 Contrasting strategic and financial appraisal

Strategic appraisal	*Financial appraisal*
• Captures a wide range of variables – both external and internal	• Focuses on a narrower range of variables – primarily internal
• Evaluation of tangible and less tangible areas of value	• Primarily concerned with tangible areas of value
• Mainly qualitative measures	• Quantitative measures
• Longer term horizons	• Bias towards shorter term (with some exceptions)
• Creative thinking	• Control process
• Deals with broader uncertainties	• Employs techniques for measuring specific risks

Table 1.1 deliberately polarises strategic and financial appraisal to highlight the key differences. It reveals that both types of appraisal appear to involve very different thinking and behavioural styles.

Yet in making major long-term financial decisions (and thus in allocating corporate resource to add to shareholder value) managers need to involve themselves in both strategic and financial appraisal. However, past research carried out in the UK by Barwise *et al*, 1988, and coordinated by London Business School indicates that managers find it extremely difficult to integrate strategic and financial appraisal when evaluating strategic decisions involving long-term financial commitment. Let us now examine why this might be the case.

There appear to be a number of factors which inhibit the linkage of strategic and financial appraisal, as follows:

- **Conceptual**: strategic appraisal typically attempts to understand how a business unit fits in totality within its external environment. By contrast, financial theory typically focuses on measuring the inherent value of a specific decision or project. Often this may occur in relative abstraction from its wider context, including the external environment and also relative to internal interdependencies.
- **Organisational**: strategic theory also suggests that organisational decision-making is a fluid, iterative and messy process. Managers make decisions based on incomplete, fragmentary and often partial views and may miss some of the wider and longer-term implications. By contrast, financial theory suggests that appraisal should be well structured, coherent and deductive. It also appears to assume that the

organisational context is steady-state or has a neutral effect on the 'rational process' of decision-making.

- **Processes:** strategic thinking is associated with planning processes and systems and also with learning from the impact of decisions on performance. By contrast, financial thinking is associated with the measurement of the most likely future performance and also with the setting up of parallel controls to track plans.

- **Systems:** strategic decisions involving long-term financial commitment may be exposed to different mixes of systems – for example strategic plans, business plans, budgets, acquisition cases and capital investment cases. This variety of systems may, therefore, be a factor causing fragmentation of vision in decision-making.

Given that the above factors explain that there is a problem, it may be worthwhile spending a few moments to draw out the implications of this problem. Table 1.2 gives some illustration of the consequences of not making effective linkages between strategic and financial appraisal, using examples from the author's past line management and consulting experience.

Table 1.2 Illustrations of some consequences of failure to link strategic and financial appraisal

Company	Linkage problem	Consequences
Computer company	Evaluation of synergies between different product streams were made on a narrowly defined, incremental basis	Synergies were counted many times over distorting the overall attractiveness of product portfolio
Financial services group	Diversification into estate agents – financial and strategic appraisal appeared to be decoupled	Heavy losses leading to divestment of this business
Technology group	Acquisition of a company on grounds of financial attractiveness – strategic benefits not well tested	Major losses leading to a turnaround exercise over three years
Telecomms company	New business opportunities were justified primarily on the basis of internal assumptions and were influenced by powerful internal sponsers	A stream of low revenue projects were launched, diluting existing profitability

Poor linkages between strategic and financial appraisal were at least partly responsible for the above problems. For example, if the value of the business strategy for the computer company had been analysed, this would have quickly highlighted the overvaluation through double-counting of internal synergies. Also, if more thorough strategic probing of the future environment for the estate agency industry had been carried out, this might at least have yielded some question marks over its 'financial attractiveness' in the latter part of the 1980s. Further, if the technology company had understood that the competitive position of the acquired company was not now sustainable (hence the owners' wish to sell) this might also have prevented such a very costly mistake. Finally, the telecomms company might have decided to curtail its costly stream of new products. This might have been achieved by working backwards from the kind of market position it was seeking to achieve in formulating its plans on how to compete, rather than juggling with the financial numbers.

This point is belaboured because history has a habit of repeating itself. These examples were not minor companies but were all within the top 200 UK companies (ranked by turnover). Even more impressive corporate failures in the early 1990s underline the problems which can arise when financial appraisal becomes unhooked from strategic appraisal, or where managers pursue a 'strategic vision' independently of financial realism. Indeed, the combination of strategic and financial appraisal within a single, unified framework offers the potential of giving extra depth of vision in the decision-making process. As in the example of everyday sight, one eye alone can only map the world in two dimensions. However, by combining strategic and financial appraisal managers gain the equivalent of two-sighted vision – thus adding a crucial, third dimension to the appraisal process.

OUR MENU OF IDEAS

So, what experiences and ideas can be brought to bear on this problem so that we can learn from past mistakes and begin to change how appraisal is undertaken? The answer is threefold:

1. This book contains a 'framework' for linking strategic and financial appraisal. This guide can be applied to making strategic decisions with major financial impact (whether these are conventionally recognised as 'investment' or not), or in evaluating a business strategy (whether this relates to a possible acquisition or divestment, or involves reappraisal of a business unit within a group). This

framework is explored in both Part 1, Chapter 4 (Linking Strategy and Financial Value) and again in Part 3, Chapter 9 (Implications).

2. This framework was tested and refined by exposure to senior managers at Rolls Royce, Grand Met (IDV), London Underground and Post Office Counters.

3. The guide also contains graphic illustrations of some specific practical problems which managers are likely to face. It also suggests ways in which these might be tackled within the five cases in Part 2 of this book, which span aeroengines, drinks, retail financial services, transportation and, finally, energy.

This illustrated guide is applicable to a wide range of strategic and financial issues and decisions and thus should be obligatory reading for:

- directors and general managers;
- operational managers;
- financial and planning managers;
- business development managers.

It should bring a number of specific benefits. It gives senior decision-makers and their advisers a 'bird's eye' view of the problem. It explains where the most difficult areas are in a way designed to strike an immediate chord with the reader. It then addresses how these problems can be approached in practice to reduce the problem of appraisal. There is also an invaluable checklist drawn from the research in Appendix 1 which will take the reader through a strategic and financial appraisal, stage by stage. This checklist can thus be tailored to your own appraisal process.

The remainder of this first part of the book now turns to:

- **Corporate strategy and longer-term financial decisions:** the tools from existing corporate strategy and theories of competitive strategy at the business level are explored to extract useful linkages with financial appraisal.
- **Financial value and longer-term financial decisions:** financial theory is summarised and then compared with research on how managers use these tools in practice, highlighting that financial theory contains only a partial account of the problem.
- **Linking strategy and financial value:** in this key chapter (4) the strands of strategic and financial theory are drawn together to distil a workable framework for linking both areas of appraisal.
- **Longer term financial decisions and the management process:** the decision-making process is explored. This highlights the problems

managers face in analysing complex strategic and financial issues in a process that is typically disjointed, often highly charged and vulnerable to political undercurrents.

REFERENCES

1. Barwise, P, Marsh, P, Thomas, K and Wensley, R (1988) *Managing Strategic Investment Decisions in Large Diversified Companies*, London Business School

2

CORPORATE STRATEGY AND LONGER-TERM FINANCIAL DECISIONS

INTRODUCTION

This chapter explores the concepts and practice of strategic appraisal of major investment decisions as follows:

- Allocating corporate resources
- Competitive analysis
- Strategic modelling theory
- Conclusions on corporate strategy

'Allocating corporate resources' describes how the allocation of investment resource can be managed through categorising the businesses in a group highlighting the strengths and weaknesses of this approach. 'Competitive analysis' then explores how strategic appraisal can be used to study the potential for value-generation at the business level. 'Strategic modelling theory' moves on to explore more quantitative techniques of evaluating a business and investment within that business. Finally, we conclude with a synthesis of those most useful insights in order to create a framework for linking strategic and financial appraisal in Chapter 4 on 'Linking Strategy and Financial Value'.

ALLOCATING CORPORATE RESOURCES

The era of the 'portfolio grid'

Whilst financial analysis tools for evaluating investment projects were being promoted vigorously through both textbooks and financial training in the 1960s and 1970s, a separate pattern of thinking on the strategic appraisal of corporate portfolios was born. In the early 1970s the idea of analysing corporate portfolios against a grid of two dimensions began to take root (for a more detailed discussion of how these relate to investment decisions, see Davidson, 1985).[1]

The most widely publicised version of the grids was that of the Boston Consulting Group (BCG). This 'growth/share matrix' or 'Boston Box' categorised any corporate portfolio into *a)* the rate of growth of demand for product or market sectors, and *b)* the relative market share of the firm (see Figure 2.1 for an illustration of the grid).

The BCG matrix has been much criticised for being too simplistic (Davidson). But the grid did represent an attempt (albeit crude) to allocate

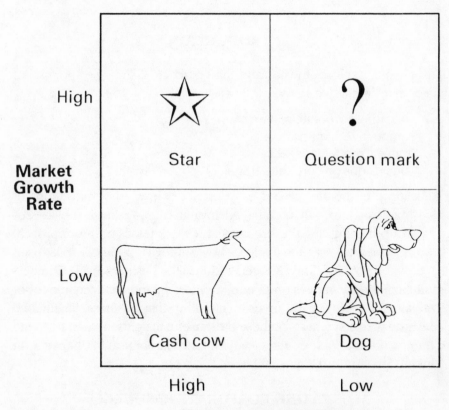

Reproduced with the kind permission of Mike Betts, Braxton Associates

Figure 2.1 The Boston Consulting Group grid

corporate investment resource according to some quasi-objective criteria, which were:

1. invest in 'stars' (high growth, high market share)
2. milk 'cash cows' (low growth, high market share)
3. divest 'dogs' (low growth, low market share)
4. monitor 'question marks' (high growth, low market share)

As a tool for appraising longer-term financial decisions the matrix appears crude in its original form because:

- growth rates are often difficult to estimate;
- relative market shares are equally difficult to estimate and beg the question of 'exactly which market (or business) are you in?';
- the grid implies that cash cows should not receive much investment – but it is often in cash cows that the greatest return from investment may be attainable;
- the grid implies that 'dogs' should be divested of, or at best, be starved of fresh investment. But in many instances 'dog' businesses may be profitable (McNamee, 1985).[2]

Despite these drawbacks, the BCG matrix remains popular with managers (as it is simple, catchy and easy to use), and with some business schools. In the author's view, however, the BCG matrix ought to carry the health warning: *Warning – the naive use of the BCG matrix can lead to inappropriate starvation of dog-like businesses and cash cows. It may also lead to inappropriate investment in 'shooting stars' that will never generate shareholder value.*

A more sophisticated attempt to use a portfolio grid tool to allocate corporate investment resources (the 'meta-level' investment decision) is the General Electric, or 'GE grid', (see Figure 2.2). The GE grid involves using two different sets of dimensions for positioning businesses within the corporate portfolio, namely industry attractiveness, and relative competitive position. Although this grid embraces a wider range of criteria than the BCG matrix and is thus easily tailored, it does have some major disadvantages.

First, to position any business on the grid demands a large amount of analysis. Both 'industry attractiveness' and 'relative competitive position' need to be evaluated according to many criteria (Davidson). Judgements on all of these multi-criteria are essentially qualitative and there is an attendant danger of loss of objectivity when using the grid.

Second, even where relative degrees of attractiveness or relative competitive position have been estimated or scored, managers then need to assess the relative importance of the various criteria in establishing an overall positioning (Tomkins, 1991).[3]

Finally the GE grid does not, in itself, enable managers to value a strategic opportunity or to compare disparate opportunities in financial terms (Tomkins), although it does provide important background data on which to base this analysis (Rappaport).[4]

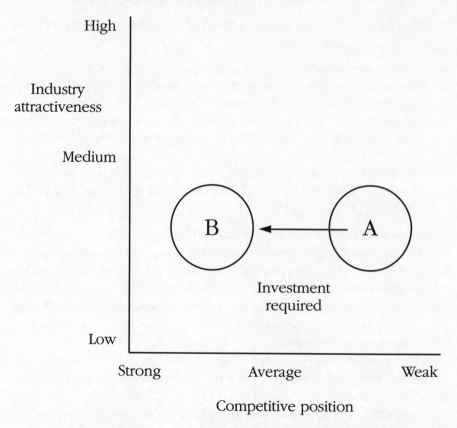

Figure 2.2 The General Electric grid

Short case study on portfolio grids – Stratech(1)

As a brief interlude, the General Electric grid (GE) was recently used during a strategic review for a large international technology company which we will call *Stratech*. The GE grid rapidly revealed a relatively high degree of ignorance concerning many of the global markets that managers were targeting. It also indicated that their competitive position was weaker than previously thought in many of these fringe markets, and that the range of targets was so wide and complex that resources were obviously being spread too thinly. In this example, therefore, the results of applying the GE grid raised a number of important strategic and financial questions which raised doubts about the competitive position of Stratech and also the inherent attractiveness of a number of its international markets.

Stratech managers also attempted to link competitive position and financial advantage by identifying:

1. the desired shift in competitive position over the period of the strategic plan (from right to left in the GE matrix, Figure 2.2);
2. the incremental improvement which this shift in competitive position would mean, *in broad financial terms*, in terms of additional revenues and level of margins;
3. the investment cost of achieving that improvement, both in capital and in non-revenue terms.

Stratech's analysis then faltered because managers got bogged down in assessing the effects (in financial terms) of improving all eight characteristics of 'competitive position', believing these to be the minimum required to shift the company's prospects. These problems highlight the difficulty of using the multi-criteria GE grid but on the other hand it suggests that managers may be tempted to shrink from recognising the full implications of strategic analysis. This would appear to be a second major barrier to strategic thinking over and above the initial barrier of understanding how to use strategic analysis tools (including the GE grid) themselves.

Conclusions

The portfolio tools alone, therefore, do not take us far forward in improving our understanding on how strategic and financial appraisal tools might be linked except in two ways. First, by indicating that the value of a longer-term financial decision *may be* impacted on by a multitude of external (as well as internal) factors, including market growth rates, relative market share and also more qualitative factors such as the stability of underlying factors driving market growth. It must also include those crucial aspects of competitive position which make competitive advantage sustainable (Rappaport). Second, by reminding us that the criteria for making a longer-term financial decision may depend not just on its apparent attractiveness as a stand-alone opportunity but also may depend on how the corporate level perceives the business unit involved. At corporate level management may thus prefer investing in one business over another where incremental returns appear similar in view of their longer-term intent for that business unit.

COMPETITIVE ANALYSIS

This section takes us into 1980s strategy theory and illustrates this thinking again with reference to the Stratech review.

The era of competitive strategy

The second major area of strategic thinking which has relevance to making major investment decisions is competitive analysis. This is more directly helpful to us in linking strategic and financial appraisal. Competitive analysis is derived from both marketing and economic thinking and was crystallised within two major works by Michael Porter – *Competitive Strategy'* (1980) and *Competitive Advantage* (1985).[5,6]

Michael Porter defines 'competitive advantage' as being the value which a firm is able to create for its customers that exceeds the firm's cost of creating it. His definition of 'value', therefore, is based on what customers are willing to pay. He also argues that the objective of competitive strategy is to create superior value either by offering lower prices than competitors for equivalent benefits or by providing unique benefits.

Key concepts of competitive analysis

Industries are dynamic: typically they go through a number of stages in their life-cycle and this changing environment has a major influence in shaping the kind of competitive strategy appropriate for a firm (Porter). During different stages of evolution there are likely to be different rates of industry profitability and varying numbers of players in the market. Towards maturity there will tend to be an increasing emphasis on cost-based competition (for example as in the early 1990s market for personal computers).

Industries also have varying structures: the degree to which an industry is 'attractive' or 'unattractive' (in terms of offering opportunities for above or below average levels of long-term profitability), according to Porter, depends on a relatively small number of factors. Porter puts forward just five – buyer power, supplier power, threat of entrants, substitutes and rivalry between existing competitors. These five factors, or competitive forces, are therefore important drivers of profitability and should be taken into account when *a)* formulating entry strategies; *b)* considering exit strategies; *c)* seeking to influence the level of profitability generally in the industry, for example, through deterring new entrants (Porter).

Strategies involve choice of positioning in these industries and how to compete and can therefore be categorised. Another key determinant of *firm* profitability is therefore the specific kind of strategy employed by it in competing against its rivals. Porter paints a picture of four types of strategy which a firm can adopt as deliberate choices. These are depicted, first of all, as a *broadly-based differentiation strategy* (eg BMW in the car industry); a *focused differentiation strategy* (eg Marks and Spencer's food business); a *broadly-based cost-leadership strategy* (eg Ford in the car industry); and finally a *focused cost-leadership strategy* (eg Tie Rack). Porter suggests that successful strategies (ie which yield above-average profits in the industry) are those which tend to be specialised, that is they follow one of the four generic, strategic alternatives. Firms which pursue a multitude of these generic strategies simultaneously tend to have average or below average profits. In Porter's words, they become 'stuck in the middle' by trying to be too many things to too many people.

Value creation of a business can be analysed as a chain of business activities. Much of *Competitive Advantage* is devoted to understanding how value is created both within the firm (value chain analysis) and also between different business units in a group (synergy analysis). The value chain is essentially a tool for understanding how value is added within a firm's operations. This is divided between those activities associated with the cycle of value creation (in-bound logistics, operations, or out-bound logistics, marketing and sales, service) and support activities. The value chain is also a useful way of thinking through not only 'what business you are in' but also 'what business *should* you be in' (and what activities generate most/least value).

Synergy both between businesses and within a business can be systematically analysed: synergy is essentially a tool for appraising the cost/benefits of linkages (tangible and less tangible) between different operational units. The value chain is again put forward by Porter as a useful tool for understanding internal linkages. Porter is also a firm advocate of the development of 'horizontal strategy' to exploit synergy within a corporate group, rather than seeing 'strategic business units' as stand-alone fighting units in the competitive battle. The reader may have noted that Porter's framework has close resemblances to the earlier GE grid. 'Industry structure' is similar to the vertical GE axis of 'industry attractiveness', whilst the horizontal axis of 'competitive position' is virtually synonymous with 'competitive advantage'.

It may also be interesting to compare Porter's concept of 'generic strategies' with the earlier prescriptions of the Boston Consulting grid. The Boston Consulting grid made a neat distinction between industry players with high market share and those with low market share, suggesting that one should, as a general rule, seek a high market share position in order to be profitable. However, Porter's concept of a 'focus' strategy acknowledges that a company can be successful by having a 'dominant' position in a particular market, segment or niche. Further, a strategy seeking 'dominance' does not necessarily require a business to have the highest market share of the segment – it can be successful simply through achieving a differentiated position.

Short case study on competitive analysis – Stratech(2)

Porter's framework was also used in the Stratech strategic review in the earlier example. A number of issues arose when applying it, as follows:

1. The 'five forces' model proved to be a very useful and rapid way of drawing out managers' views of the current environment. What proved far more difficult, however, was stretching this thinking beyond the next two years. This involved exploring uncertainties of technology change, the shape of market development, competitor activity and also of deregulation. These uncertainties compounded further into the future.
2. Competitor analysis was an invaluable way of testing in-company views on competitive position. By asking a relatively small number of key customers and target customers how they saw Stratech it proved possible to shift views of existing competitive strengths and weaknesses. The early 'SWOT' analysis conducted by management proved to be unrealistic. But again, competitor analysis proved difficult to project into the future to cover possible competitor intent.
3. Value chain analysis enabled management to isolate the small number of products which made the bulk of Stratech's profits. This raised issues about whether investment in newer, higher growth areas diluted profits as market share was being won at lower gross margins. These innovatory products were also in areas where Stratech's competitive position was not so strong.
4. The idea of 'generic strategies' especially of cost leadership caused difficulties. First, managers had to move away from the idea of

'differentiation' as simply 'being different'. Second, managers did not appreciate readily that being a 'cost leader' meant being *the* lowest cost player. Besides difficulties in conceptual understanding, there was a strong emotional reaction against the idea of 'cost leadership' generally, even though this was renamed, more palatably, a 'best cost' strategy. Managers believed this cost-led strategy implied that it meant 'we pile it high and sell it cheap', even though this was not part of the strategy. This reaction to a 'best cost' strategy was despite the fact that very often Stratech's behaviour was in that mode in the market place.

The Stratech strategic review raises some interesting questions on the effectiveness of strategic thinking generally. Strategic thinking is affected very much by an organisation's self-concept of 'how we do things around here' not only in terms of operational routines but also in the use of financial planning and control systems (its 'paradigm'). Any change to appraisal processes must take into account how this impacts on the rituals, routines and symbols at work in the decision making process.

Finally, possibly even more bite could have been put into Stratech's review simply by sharper *financial* quantification of competitive options. Managers preferred to evaluate these primarily using qualitative criteria rather than to subject them to rigorous and detailed quantitative analysis. This suggests also that in order to forge closer links between strategic and financial appraisal it is necessary to have already in place a reasonably well established and vision-led strategic planning process.

Key benefits of competitive analysis

To summarise the attractions of competitive analysis, we can conclude that competitive analysis provides a relatively comprehensive framework for understanding *a)* the external, competitive environment; *b)* the internal environment of a firm; and *c)* provides help on how to understand that external and internal analysis can be linked in the strategic appraisal.

Competitive analysis also helps focus strategic analysis on understanding how value is created under competitive market conditions, both externally and internally. It stresses the need to understand not only the dynamics and structure of these markets as a competitive process, but also how to check or test the strategic analysis through financial appraisal. For example, key financial tests of an 'attractive market or industry' are that it yields above-average profits relative to other industries (and thus performance is sustained long-term). Also, the test of a genuine differentiation strategy is that the firm achieves a clear price premium for its products and services. Likewise the test of a cost leadership strategy is that, literally, the company's products and services are produced at *the lowest cost* in the industry.

Another key benefit of competitive analysis is that it suggests that strategic appraisal should embrace *competitors' strategies* rather than focusing purely on the growth prospects or general attractiveness of particular products and markets, the latter of which results in competitive myopia.

The idea of 'competitive advantage' has great simplicity and appeal (almost like the idea of an NPV – a single, simple measure of value – for financial appraisal). This provides a powerful vehicle for communicating simple linkages between strategic and financial appraisal within an organisation.

Illustrating competitive and financial linkages – Porter's Skil Case

It may also be useful to further illustrate the above attractions with reference to Porter's own Harvard case on the Skil Corporation, which was used as a core tool to highlight managers' problems and perceptions in the cases in Chapters 6 and 7.

In this case Michael Porter is depicted on video in conversation with the CEO of Skil. Emerson, who purchased Skil Corporation in the early 1980s, quickly found that the business, that of producing and selling a range of electrical tools worldwide, required a turnaround. During the 1980s, Skil refocused its strategy to concentrate on a narrower range of distribution channels which it would exploit via cost leadership. This involved radical simplification of its products and manufacturing operations in parallel with major investment in new manufacturing technology and in repositioning its market image.

During the video, Porter highlights the time lag of several years between commencement of a strategic turnaround and the harvesting of benefits in financial performance. He expresses wonder at the relationship between 'strategic' and 'financial' health of a company, marvelling at how apparent financial health can obscure strategic decline, and that strategic improvement can be marred by sluggish improvement in financial performance.

This video was also shown to senior managers at Stratech during their strategic review. There were some sharp intakes of breath as managers saw the very close parallels with their own efforts to regenerate financial performance through, in effect, a 'strategic turnaround'. Indeed, at one stage I thought Stratech's director of business development was about to have a seizure. (Frequently managers embark on a strategy to pursue growth when the business is actually facing competitive decline and in need of medium-term turnaround.) However, at Stratech, although managers made ready connections between strategic and financial appraisal off-site in a workshop process, they faced major barriers in feeding these lessons back into the management process. Even though close parallels between Skil and Stratech were raised with the top management team, it proved hard for the team to digest the full implications, not so much because of analysis difficulties but more because of the major issues of strategic change which they suggested.

This again demonstrates the influence of management behaviour on the formal and informal appraisal process which we shall explore in greater depth in Chapter 5.

Although the Skil case poses some difficult questions on linking strategic and financial appraisal, Porter unfortunately fails to enlighten us on the processes that might be at work here. These might include, for example:

- internal lags in communicating a revised strategy and in formulating plans to implement change and in carrying these plans out;
- external lags in changing the perceptions of customers and distribution channels;
- the effects of absolute versus relative change: customer expectations, competitors and technology processes do not stay still. In order to translate strategic improvement generally into improved financial performance it is likely that the effect of *relative* rather than *absolute* change is the key variable;
- improvement may need to be of a critical mass and of a quantum amount to generate sufficient improvement in cost or value, otherwise a virtuous cycle of financial improvement will not begin;
- the effects of underlying improvement in strategic health may be masked – for example through a recession (as at Stratech) – or in Skil's case, by adverse currency movements.

Key drawbacks of competitive analysis

From our review of competitive analysis a number of practical limitations of Porter's framework emerge:

1. Porter's framework is very comprehensive, resulting in large data requirements for strategic analysis. This may well result in overload for managers seeking to apply these tools in practice. (This is borne out by the earlier example of Stratech.)

2. Although Porter draws some linkages between strategic and financial analysis these are made only at a very broad level. Although he is clearly very interested in the relationships between strategic and financial appraisal, he appears not to have addressed the more detailed linkages which might exist.

3. When Porter mentions the topic of 'investment' this is either as *a)* a determinant of entry barriers within the industry structure; or *b)* as an incidental ingredient within the overall competitive strategy. Porter's theory, therefore, appears to be concerned primarily with market positioning and the alignment of resource within that positioning rather than with injecting strategic vision into the making of longer-term financial decisions. These decisions, taken as a 'set' as in the Skil case, may combine, however, in creating sustainable competitive advantage, although there is no reason why Porter's framework of competitive analysis cannot be tailored to help the appraisal of longer-term financial decisions to be more outwardly focused. Indeed, in the earlier Stratech case, a major barrier was that the focus of the strategic review was primarily on market development and that 'investment' was perceived as a more secondary issue. Subsequently the Stratech review ran into difficulties precisely because the size and nature of investment required to implement the strategy was not 'sold' for its strategic and financial benefits to Group Head Office.

4. Finally, Porter's generic recommendations may appear plausible precisely because they are generalised prescriptions and therefore abstract from the ambiguity and uncertainty which surrounds longer-term financial decisions. This is a major concern in the four core cases in Chapters 6 and 7.

On the positive side, Porter's emphasis in value creation begins to draw much closer linkages between strategic and financial appraisal than that which we saw in corporate portfolio theory. Although his work on linking strategic and financial appraisal primarily concerned planning processes in general, much of his framework can be applied to the making of longer-term financial decisions. Often these decisions can play a central role in shaping strategy development in practice (see Chapter 5).

MODELLING THE STRATEGY

In parallel with portfolio theory (1970s) and competitive analysis (1980s), another important strand is 'modelling the strategy'. This includes modelling of the relationships between strategic, operational and variables of businesses, either to compare the performance of different businesses or to understand how value is created within a particular business.

Modelling techniques derive from three sources: economics, statistics and computing. A major factor enabling strategic modelling has been computer-based forecasting. This is complemented by databases for capturing, analysis and manipulation of strategic, operational and financial data. These approaches fall into two main categories:

- Empirically-derived models which are calibrated with reference to how businesses have performed in the past, particularly the PIMS ('Profit Impact of Marketing Strategy') database.
- Decision-support tools geared to representing the strategic position of a business and its impact on operational and financial variables and vice versa.

The PIMS database

The PIMS database is a leading example of the first type of approach. This is run by the Strategic Planning Institute (based in London in the UK) and contains performance data from a large number of companies across many industries. Not only does it contain return on investment (ROI) data, but also data on market share, R&D, on quality and other measures.

The PIMS computer database indicated that there appeared to be a strong, positive correlation between having a high relative market share and also having a higher than average level of profitability across a variety of industries. A number of other variables were found to be statistically significant predictors of above average profitability, including, for example, the relative quality of products and services, and also the level of investment intensity. Curiously, investment intensity was found to be *inversely proportional* to relative profitability – where investment is high, returns are typically depressed. No doubt this is due to the problems of over-investment or the ineffective use of investment in many industries.

The PIMS database is claimed to be particularly useful in giving managers an objective test on their strategic planning assumptions for a particular business unit (Buzzell and Gale, 1987).[7] Using PIMS it is possible to 'reality-test' managers' assumptions on the likely profit stream resulting from a business. This is done by comparing it with 'look-alike' businesses. Data on look-alikes are extracted from the PIMS database. Typically these look-alikes may be in other industries, but with comparable features, and this can highlight managers' unrealistic expectations, or alternatively show that there may be untapped potential for improving returns.

The PIMS database was used primarily to look at determinants of return on capital employed or 'investment' (an accounting-based measure) for an entire business unit. Buzzell and Gale described how PIMS can be used where managers are considering making a major business investment decision, especially to 'reality-test' managers' assumptions. The PIMS database can also be used to compile discounted-cash-flow-based assessments for an investment project or for a business, rather than merely profit-based measures.

PIMS also highlights that realised returns on investment are often much lower than expected returns. This might be because managers were simply being over-optimistic, or because of difficulties in the definition of cash flows which are incremental to that project.

Business modelling

Turning next to the use of economic/computing models, Simmonds (1984)[8] suggests that strategic analysis should have close links with management accounting (or what Simmonds calls 'strategic management accounting' – SMA). SMA brings together a number of strategic and financial techniques, namely experience curve analysis and interdependencies between pricing strategies and market share. SMA also examines the effect of competitor response to strategic moves and the impact on industry structure from increasing capacity by a number of players.

Although Simmonds' work is a useful example of how modelling approaches may be interrelated, his worked illustrations are inevitably simplified (for example, one depicts only three, well-defined competitors in an industry – an unlikely situation in reality).

Other approaches include that of modelling the impact of competitor reaction on a return on investment from a particular strategy. This may take the form of doing 'what if' analysis to identify the effects of entry by a new competitor. 'Competitor reaction sensitivities' may provide a powerful antidote to the tendency for managers to exhibit 'competitive myopia' as identified earlier. A problem with modelling approaches, however, is of choosing amongst a number of possible scenarios, all of which may seem equally plausible. As the modelling problem becomes more complex the 'number' of scenarios can multiply, making it hard for managers to pick their way through the complexity. This may explain why managers' experimentation with strategic modelling appears limited. For example, managers appear to have been slow to exploit the potential of competitor intelligence in the UK, yet this is essential in order to assess likely *competitor intent* which may be an important variable impacting on financial value.

By way of illustration, I was involved in a major project to explore competitor positioning in the financial services industry which involved the development of a large database to analyse a company's competitive position. This absorbed many months' effort of both internal management and that of a consultancy team, yet little, if any, attempt was made to explore the *future* intent of major competitors. Arguably, this was at least as important as the existing positioning of competitors. Future competitor intent was probably a decisive factor in determining the value of decisions aimed at reshaping this business' future development. The lesson from this exercise is that managers need to look beyond the most tangible variables towards underlying factors including competitor intent, which may provide broad indicators of whether 'value' will be harvested as anticipated.

Model-based approaches of the above kind seek to *reduce* the information overload facing managers through *a)* well-structuring of a complex problem, and, *b)* using computing power to alleviate the difficulties of information overload. However, this gives rise to the following problems:

- In order to well-structure the problem either a very large number of variables have to be built in, resulting in highly complex interrelationships, or, alternatively, the model may become merely an oversimplified representation of reality and fail to capture major uncertainties.
- Some of the key data parameters may not be readily set – for example highly uncertain variables like 'competitor reaction or intent' as we have already seen. Trying to resolve this through further development of modelling subsystems and by databases of information may not resolve the fundamental problem that much of the data is 'soft' and requires a more flexible, judgmental approach by managers.
- Complex data modelling tools may result ultimately in *less* rather than *greater* insight by managers as the appraisal problem becomes artificially mechanised and perhaps over detailed. Models may thus run into the trap of becoming 'black boxes' into which managers pour assumptions. The model then manipulates these assumptions in ways

which are complex and not immediately evident to produce outputs in which managers therefore have low intuitive confidence. This may take away an important source of 'soft logic' and also of confidence and commitment building – managers' judgement.

Although model or simulation-based approaches may be useful for relatively well structured problems, for less well structured problems, such as the making of major financial decisions under conditions of uncertainty, these approaches, therefore, have significant practical drawbacks.

CONCLUSIONS ON CORPORATE STRATEGY

The key conclusions of this chapter for linking strategic and financial appraisal can be summarised as follows:

- The BCG matrix is a crude way of allocating corporate investment resource and can lead to inappropriate choices in resource allocation.
- The GE Grid may give a more refined picture of key investment opportunities and help to position business units, but is demanding in data requirements. It may also require gathering and evaluating a large amount of qualitative data as a basis for management judgement. This is likely to present managers with problems when seeking to draw out the quantitative, financial implications of 'softer' analysis.
- Competitive analysis provides a more focused set of tools for thinking about linking strategic and financial appraisal, but again appears to be too broadly pitched. Porter's framework appears to be tailored closely to evaluating cash flows of an entire business. However, with some further tailoring it may be possible to apply it to the level of a specific strategic decision in such a way as to link in with financial appraisal.
- Strategic modelling approaches may seem to offer advantages in quantifying the value of a major investment decision or a strategic business unit in financial terms. Dealing with database approaches, PIMS has a long established track record and may well shed useful light through 'reality-testing' managers' financially-orientated assumptions. PIMS requires working closely with an external body (the Strategic Planning Institute) to run the PIMS database. Also, unless modelling approaches are *a)* flexible; *b)* stimulate rather than close-down creative and insightful thinking by managers; and *c)* do not try to remove the element of management judgement, then they may hamper rather than facilitate effective decision-making.

This discussion of strategic appraisal is not yet complete as we will be turning to ideas of competitive theories of value creation and of 'shareholder value' in Chapter 4.

REFERENCES

1. Davidson, K (1985) 'Strategic Investment Theories', *The Journal of Business Strategy*, vol 6, no 1, pp 16-28, Summer
2. McNamee, PB (1985) *Tools and Techniques for Strategic Management*, Pergamon, Oxford
3. Tomkins, C (1991) *Corporate Resource Allocation – Financial, Strategic and Organisational Perspectives*, Basil Blackwell, Oxford
4. Rappaport, A (1987) 'Linking Competitive Strategy and Shareholder Value Analysis', *The Journal of Business Strategy*, vol 7, no 4, pp 58-67, Spring
5. Porter, M E (1980) *Competitive Strategy*, The Free Press, Macmillan, New York
6. Porter, M E (1985) *Competitive Advantage*, The Free Press, Macmillan, New York
7. Buzzell, R D and Gale, B T (1987) *The PIMS Principles*, The Free Press, Macmillan, New York
8. Simmonds, K (1984) *The Accounting Assessment of Competitive Position*, London Business School Paper

3

FINANCIAL VALUE AND LONGER-TERM FINANCIAL DECISIONS

INTRODUCTION

Over the past thirty years or so, financial appraisal techniques have played an influential role in both academic thinking and in management practice concerning major investment decisions. This appeal may be due to the inherent simplicity of its core prescriptions and to its theoretical rigour and elegance. It is also eminently 'teachable' (and thus examinable) through MBA programmes and in financial training generally which has no doubt played some role in its wide dissemination to managers. Its popularity may also be due in part to its power as a 'management comforter'. A cynical view might be that it is akin perhaps to a corporate Valium in its ability to numb the decision-taker against the uncertainty in the decision process.

An unexpected visitor from the planet Venus could be forgiven for becoming confused if he were to embark on a research study of longer-term financial decisions. What he/she (or indeed 'it') would read in corporate finance books might bear little resemblance to what actually happens in practice. For our extra-terrestrial visitor, financial theory would appear both clear and comprehensive on how to appraise investment decisions. Perhaps he might initially refer to the comprehensive framework for financial appraisal as contained in Brealey and Myers (1984).[1] Their core approach embraces the concept that financial theory aims at arriving at a measure of the *value* of a particular longer-term financial decision. It therefore provides a means of trading off a mélange of benefits, costs and risks associated with any longer-term financial decision.

The theory and practice of financial theory is now illustrated (with examples from the Cranfield research) as follows:

- What we are investing in?
- Finding the tools
- The cost of investing
- Defining the stream of cash flows.

WHAT ARE WE INVESTING IN?

Most textbooks on corporate finance tell us that the *investment project* is the primary unit of analysis. For financial literature the 'project' is typically considered to be a 'given' for the purposes of analysis. This may imply to the unaware manager that there is relatively little need to reshape the project through ongoing analysis or a need to understand the project in its broader context.

Also, the typical object of analysis is an investment decision in *tangible* assets. Much of the financial literature seems to assume that we are talking about capital investment decisions – that is, investment decisions whose initial outlay will become capitalised on the company's balance sheet. Indeed the appraisal process is often called 'capital budgeting' (King, 1975).[2] In the Cranfield research, although 'capital' investment was a major focus for internal appraisal, managers were also concerned about how to evaluate less tangible areas of investment including image, brands, and acquisitions (which exhibit a mix of tangible and less tangible value) through to revenue costs such as training. For instance, IDV (a major division of Grand Met) spends more on developing brands such as Smirnoff or Malibu than it does on capital investment.

Financial theory therefore suggests that the unit of analysis for investment decisions, and indeed what actually 'is' an investment decision, is relatively uncontentious and unproblematic. Later on we will see that in practice this is far from being the case. The four Cranfield cases suggested that managers focus primarily on appraising investment at the project-by-project level rather than at the business level (although at Rolls Royce and Post Office Counters, DCF appraisal was also extended to higher business or corporate level strategy).

King also provides an earlier account of the appraisal process involved in making major investment decisions. This identified a series of stages which an investment decision might typically go through. King suggested that after the initial stage of 'screening' of a multiplicity of opportunities, companies then characteristically define a specific project to be appraised (the 'definition' phase). King suggests that 'at the screening stage the precise form of a project will be vague'. Although King's three cases imply that managers usually consider at most only one or two alternatives to the project, they do not yield insights about how the 'project' is defined in relation to other projects in the business, nor do other surveys (for example, Pike and Dobbins, 1984).[3]

In the Cranfield research, the definition of the 'project' and the 'unit of analysis' was often far from self-evident. For example, one manager from Post Office Counters describes refurbishment as follows:

> It is not a consistent approach. We have some things which we have done well and then there is a tatty old writing desk there. We ought to do the security, everything else, all at one go. It doesn't strike me as particularly difficult. Alright, you have got to co-ordinate a number of people.

The above example highlights that the prescriptions of financial theory on defining the project are reinforced by the functional viewpoints of managers.

FINDING THE TOOLS

Financial theory stresses that the value of an investment decision can only be derived from measuring *cash flows* rather from accounting-based measures such as 'return on investment' (ROI). For investment in an existing business the appropriate cash flows to be measured are deemed to be those which are *incremental* to the decision.

The core problems of valuing an opportunity are seen as residing in the existence of both risk and of the time lag between outlays and recouping cash inflows.

First, risk; most business investment decisions involve some degree of risk – the investor may recoup either more or less than his original investment plus anticipated return. We may believe (on an intuitive basis) that an investor may prefer to invest in an opportunity with lower return if the business-related risk involved is proportionately lower, but this is contradicted by theory. Financial theory argues that it is up to investors, not managers, to diversify risk, (although the latter should nevertheless *reduce* the impact of project-specific risk on cash flows as far as is practicable). Financial theory also argues that any fair appreciation of the value of an investment decision needs to reflect some adjustment for the declining value of money over time, both to compensate for inflation and to obtain a real rate of return. The provision of capital to a business over time is regarded as not being 'free' but having a definite 'cost', rather like that of a rent. Financial theory suggests, therefore, that the cash flow stream associated with an investment should then be 'discounted'. The impact of discounting is described in greater length in Appendix 3.

Discount rates can be used to test a cash flow stream to identify its net present value (NPV) at a particular 'cost of capital' (which we will be covering shortly). The NPV is the present value of the future cash flows less the investment outlay – this is a measure of the value added by an investment in economic terms. Alternatively managers can calculate the discount rate at which the NPV is zero, or the 'internal rate of return' (IRR). In many ways the IRR is easier to understand than NPV as it enables managers to compare projects in a way which is more accessible. However, there are dangers in opting for a project just because it has a high IRR. This might prevent managers from going ahead with a project which adds larger *absolute value*, even though its IRR is lower. This is amplified in the Rolls Royce example later on in the chapter. Also, there are dangers that managers may confuse the IRR with Return on Investment or ROI, the latter of which is based on measurement of income streams based on accounting adjustments, not on cash flows.

Although NPV is generally agreed in the financial literature to be the best economic measure of the value of a business investment rather than IRR or payback, there may be considerable barriers against using it effectively. One is that most management control processes are derived from accounting-based measurements rather than incremental cash flow. For many, if not most, companies these financial control mechanisms are extremely powerful in shaping decision-making. Also, NPV may be inherently difficult to understand and may therefore present managers with a learning curve not easy to surmount.

Empirical studies indicate that managers do seek to derive *incremental* analyses of the cash flows from major investment decisions. But based on their fieldwork, Barwise *et al* (1988)[4] point out that the question of 'incremental on what?' is not so well addressed. Barwise *et al* also highlight that managers face significant problems in deciding what benefits and costs should be 'in' or 'out' of the proposal. Following their study of investment decision-making in a small number of companies, they concluded that investment cases were typically sets of projections which gave *just enough* justification for projects. Project 'upsides' may often be held back so that managers can keep some value, as it were, 'up their sleeves'.

Research on how managers use these tools tells us that:

- Accounting-based measures of return, including return on investment or ROI, are still used by many managers, even though these are not prescribed by financial theory as appropriate.

- Payback, which is considered by financial theory as being the *least* theoretically sound tool, still plays a major role in many organisations. The Cranfield research highlighted that payback was in regular use with the caveat that payback can encourage too many 'tactical projects' (especially at Post Office Counters Limited).
- Internal rate of return (IRR) is also used extensively by managers. Although IRR makes use of discounted cash flow techniques, many financial textbooks consider it inferior to NPV. Again, in the Cranfield research IRR was popular and in some cases dominated over NPV.
- NPV is the *least* popular measure of all, despite its primacy in financial theory, although its popularity has increased somewhat over the last twenty years.

Besides the issue of what techniques are in use is the further issue of whether these techniques are fully understood and properly applied by management. Pike's survey appears to suggest that managers had become less prone to technical error in using NPV by the early 1980s. But in 1988 Barwise *et al* discovered that some serious analytical errors might occur due to managers confusing profit measurement and cash flows, being unclear on how to derive an appropriate discount rate, and through inconsistent assessment of terminal values. These inherent dangers are also illustrated in the Cranfield research. For example at one company in this research it was highlighted that:

> I had an amusing situation . . . the finance person said to me, 'I don't like NPVs because I don't understand them; I prefer to look at IRRs' and so we went back to the computer to churn out the IRRs. And there were certain cash flows which were very strange – we got to the number 2,580 per cent [laughter]. We decided to stop.

In the above case the manager already appreciated the mechanical pitfalls of IRR and was able to steer his colleagues out of this problem.

These problems were echoed by another manager in one of three other cases:

> It is a . . . the IRR and discounted cash flow. I get confused about what it is telling me. What happens if I do an IRR and I don't think I am sophisticated enough? I don't think I have enough knowledge of the techniques to say 'these are the differences' and 'this is how it will make the decision-taking process better.'

He also went on to raise the question 'How do we actually get to IRRs for acquisitions? I get the impression that it is between 15 per cent and 20 per cent – we use 20 per cent where it is high risk. How do we get there?' This contrasts sharply with the attractions of payback to managers. The same manager tells us: 'Payback, for all its weaknesses, is nice and simple' (for capital investment).

Another issue is just how important financial measures are vis-à-vis non-financial or qualitative measures, especially where cash flows are either inherently difficult to define, or are particularly uncertain. Pike and Dobbins suggest that qualitative factors *do* play a major role in the judgements made by managers. Again, Pike's study does not seek to explore why or how qualitative factors are perceived to be important by management, whether qualitative factors are partially or wholly amenable to quantification, or how they are or might be dealt with throughout the decision process.

Although these more technical issues are significant, this book does not seek to explore comprehensively the technical advantages and disadvantages of these differing financial tools. These are dealt with exhaustively in classic text books (for example, Brealey and Myers). There is also a significant danger of mistaking this as being *the* core appraisal problem – whereas it is merely one of many. Managers need to be aware of the analytical pitfalls of these measures but they also need to be reminded that these may pale into insignificance against others which are frequently more difficult to resolve. These might include, for instance, the appraisal of intangible value, the assessment of uncertainty (whether this has upsides or downsides) and also how to tackle the 'do nothing' or base case. In addition, there are contentious issues over how to manage the appraisal process itself (see Chapter 5).

THE COST OF INVESTING

A key concern for financial theory has been the derivation and use of a firm's 'cost of capital'. Most modern financial textbooks suggest that the cost of capital should be derived from Capital Asset Pricing theory or CAPM. According to CAPM, the cost of capital for a company is the risk-free rate plus a variable increment. This is the incremental difference between the expected return on the stock market as a whole, less the risk-free rate which is then *multiplied by* a variable factor. This variable factor is specific to that corporate entity, and is named (almost as if to confuse the average manager) a 'Beta'.

CAPM suggests that the higher the value of Beta then the higher the required rate of return for those investment stocks and therefore the higher the cost of investing in a particular corporation. For the mathematical reader, $K_e = R_f + B(R_m - R_f)$ where:

K_e is the cost of capital
R_f is the risk free rate
R_m is the expected return on the stock market
and B (or 'Beta') is a constant for the firm.

What the above is saying, therefore, is simply this – that the higher a company's 'Beta', the higher its cost of capital will be (the 'risk free' rate is common between investment stocks at a particular point of time). To find out the Beta, it is possible to deduce the premium or discount which shareholders put on a company by empirical study. To save managers' time and trouble, it is possible to ascertain Beta for a particular company from specialist sources, such as the London Business School. But even this can cause problems – one view being that Betas do not diverge greatly between different kinds of Groups (Fielding, 1989).[5]

Again, this book resists the temptation to explore in depth technical features associated with financial theory and it is not proposed to enter into a detailed debate of CAPM. There are practical difficulties associated with estimating Beta as it is necessary to identify what industry sector a company belongs to – this is not always self-evident, especially for conglomerates. Later work has suggested that these difficulties are not insuperable (Copeland *et al*, 1990),[6] as it may be possible to assess a weighted average of Beta by analysing each division separately within a group.

CAPM may also be counter-intuitive to managers, for example in its suggesting that diversification is not a justifiable objective for a business strategy. Modern Financial Theory (or 'MFT') suggests that corporate diversification, which is aimed at spreading corporate risks, does not benefit shareholders, as they can diversify their portfolio of securities themselves. This idea appears not well understood by many managers. Yet diversification of risk may often be a rationalisation for strategic moves aimed at bolstering managers' own security of tenure, rather than for protecting shareholder value. Risk minimisation of this kind is not to be confused with securing benefits by reducing operational risk. For example, it may be possible, by adding an activity related to the current business, to reduce the risk of operations running at below normal levels of activity. Such a project may therefore add value. But the means of evaluating this (according to financial theory) should be to incorporate a value for this operational flexibility explicitly in the appraisal. This would require assumptions on the likelihood of running at low levels of throughput without the additional project.

In summary, therefore, there are some significant difficulties associated with defining the cost of capital for the purpose of appraising major investment decisions. However, some of these difficulties may be regarded as 'splitting hairs' as the cost of investing (the 'cost of capital') is merely one variable in computing net present value. The relative importance of the cost of capital will vary depending upon the length of time over which investment cash flows may be recouped. On reflection, one is mindful of thinking of the mystical aura surrounding CAPM as indicating that 'CAPM' might really stand for 'Capital Asset Produces Mystique'.

Practical financial measures

Turning next to financial measures which managers use in practice, we have already seen that managers have difficulty in selecting and using the appropriate financial measurement tools for the job. These difficulties are compounded by the need to decide the rate of discounting which reflects the appropriate cost of capital. These problems fall into two main areas; first the selection of an appropriate 'cost of capital', and second the application of this 'cost of capital' to a series of investment opportunities (the 'capital budgeting' process).

Results of past research:

Previous research carried out reveals that managers use a very wide range of costs of capital in evaluating major investment decisions, and often use very high hurdle rates. These penal rates might be due either to *a)* ignorance about the 'true' cost of capital, *b)* adjustment for risk premiums, or *c)* adjustment to compensate for management bias towards over-optimism. Further, managers may appear to make arbitrary changes in hurdle rates. This misapplication of financial tools has been one factor leading to a school of financial theory known as 'behavioural finance'.

The selection of 'cost of capital' based on explicit use of models of financial theory (eg the CAPM) appears to be the exception rather than the rule. Managers often devise a cost of capital based on extremely crude calculations – for example, using the cost of bank borrowing and adding a premium for risk. The Cranfield research found that in all four cases there was a degree of ambiguity about the basis for cost of capital. Yet this is an area about which managers do seem to be very concerned. For example, one manager in this research said: 'It was reassuring to hear that they agreed with us – everyone said X%.'

Once selected, the cost of capital is sometimes used for relatively long periods of time without review, although the frequency of review appears to have increased since the 1970s (Pike).

Research also showed that the cost of capital is seen as the *financial hurdle* – once over the hurdle then the project is given the green light automatically where no artificial capital rationing prevails (Barwise *et al*). This implies that a firm can fund any project which comes along as long as it has a positive NPV – regardless of its cash flow profile or commitments to other projects. ('Capital rationing' means that there are absolute constraints in the *amount* of finance available for investment regardless of the opportunities available).

Finally there were indications that where capital is perceived to be rationed, managers face significant problems in dealing with the use of 'cost of capital'. This is because they find that if they let it operate unhindered it will allow too many projects to 'jump over the hurdle'. This may encourage the step of simply raising the test discount rate or 'hurdle'. The cases in Chapters 6 and 7 suggest that decision criteria *are* typically variable – and that the basis of variation is not always transparent to managers themselves.

Unfortunately previous research does not shed much light on how widespread 'capital rationing' is, but managers are likely to perceive themselves to be almost invariably constrained by the amount of 'investment' or 'capital' programmes which can be afforded. Large-scale investment (even where it is defined as 'capital') generates additional charges to profits through both depreciation and interest, thus lowering reported earnings. Pressure to maintain reported earnings (on an accounting basis) was found to be important in all four cases (see Chapters 6 and 7).

DEFINING THE STREAM OF CASH FLOWS

The following is a guide to estimating incremental cash flows. Financial textbooks such as Brealey and Myers deal with this subject in much greater detail.

A quick guide for managers and off-planet visitors to financial evaluation

The following steps are required:

- Existing cash inflows and outflows of the business are projected into the future.
- The *incremental* cash flows arising over time from the investment are then estimated.

- A risk assessment of these incremental cash flows is performed in order to test sensitivities (but *not* as a basis for raising the hurdle rate).
- The incremental cash flows (net of tax) are then discounted to adjust for:
  - the time value of money (to compensate investors for deferring their own cash stream into the future);
  - the relative level of 'risk' as measured by either the group's 'beta' or preferably the equivalent beta for the division;
  - the impact of financial gearing (again see financial textbooks for more detail of the mechanics)
- The present value of future cash flows less initial investment outlays is called the 'NPV'.

'Relevant' cash flows

Financial theory prescribes careful definition of 'incremental' cash flows to ensure that only those truly 'relevant' to the decision are included. This involves for example avoiding the use of sunk costs (ie costs which have already been incurred or are committed and unavoidable). It also involves incorporating cash flows which may not be instantly regarded as being linked to the project, for example, working capital requirements.

However, financial theory defines those cash flows which are 'relevant' to the decision to be a matter of internal analysis focusing on the investment project itself. Theory also goes as far as suggesting that the economist's opportunity cost should be incorporated. But this is not an obvious and easy area for managers to implement, however, as managers need to stand back and ask themselves about the alternative use of resources. But in some situations *opportunity cost* does yield some interesting insights. For example, in one company which I advised, there were major constraints in scarce technical skills, and the imputed value of a particular specialist ran to millions of pounds. This raised questions about the wisdom of policy constraints *not* to subcontract technical work.

Financial theory also assumes that the project is more or less already well defined and is a 'given' for financial analysis (King). This has two key implications; first, the opportunity is assumed to be clear cut and therefore financial appraisal is seen as being merely a measurement exercise, and second any uncertainties can be handled effectively by risk and/or sensitivity analysis.

Financial theory also appears to suggest that the choice of which key assumptions managers should consider within the presentation of any business case is largely self-evident (with the exception of related theory on statistical analysis). With very few exceptions, textbooks on corporate finance are often presented as if they contain a self-contained and complete answer to the problem of evaluating longer-term financial decisions. A recent counter example (Copeland *et al*) emphasises the need to check that assumptions for a project need to be tested against the underlying competitive position and the likely sustainability of its cash flows, but this is an island in the large expanse of financial theory.

According to financial theory, incremental cash flow is the difference between cash flows on a 'with-investment' basis versus cash flows on a 'without the investment' basis. The latter view is sometimes called the 'base case' (for example by Barwise *et al*). Financial theory appears to regard the base case as unproblematic. Although not stated explicitly in the theory, financial textbooks can easily infer to managers that the 'base case' represents a steady-state view of the world. We shall see later on (Chapters 6 and 7) that there are many instances where a steady-state base case may be the exception, rather than the rule.

Financial theory has also identified a number of problems in defining the 'with investment case':

- Forecasting the effects on variables which enhance competitive position and which may, therefore, indirectly result in increased volumes, better prices or lower costs (Simmonds, 1984;[7] Kaplan, 1986[8]).
- Problems of apportioning cash flows to projects which are inter-dependent (Coulthurst and Sizer, 1984).[9]
- Defining the most appropriate time horizons for forecasts: this links into the problem of estimating terminal values or the presumed value of the investment decision at the end of more detailed projections (Copeland, Koller and Murrin).
- Dealing with a number of uncertain variables which interact with one another, for example, sales revenues, unit costs and investment outlays. This is often associated with managers erroneously hiking the discount rates as blanket compensation for risk.
- Valuing opportunities whose value may or may not be harvested in the future (eg the creation of spin-off opportunities or the value of penetrating a market with very uncertain growth prospects). These opportunities are highly contingent but are an important factor in justifying the investment.

Each of these issues is now dealt with in turn.

Apportionment difficulties

First, dealing with problems of apportionment, it may be difficult, if not impossible, to apportion cash flows to a project which is linked closely with others. Certain investments may be highly interdependent with others. This may suggest that the level of analysis might be taken as being a set of projects, rather than as a single project in isolation. Kaplan (1987)[10] also argues that in many instances the *cost data* upon which an investment appraisal may depend may be misleading, especially in the treatment of 'fixed costs' which may be of a variable or semi-variable nature.

Coulthurst (1986)[11] also suggests that the effect of infrastructure (for example, IT systems, Head Office investment) can be compensated for by making an adjustment to the hurdle cost of capital. By increasing this hurdle it is possible to force a business to invest in 'productive' investment projects at sufficiently high rates of return to compensate for the cost of its supporting infrastructure and to generate a return above its cost of capital. However this method of increasing the discount rate and applying this to the cash flows from directly productive investment appears to be very crude. There is no guarantee that increasing the hurdle rate for new projects which happen to be 'productive financially' will generate sufficient present value to cover the additional infrastructure involved. Raising the discount rate is a very hit and miss approach to compensating for this, as Table 3.1 shows.

Table 3.1   The effect of raising the discount rate

	A *10% discount rate (£M)*	B *15% discount rate (£M)*
Present value of infrastructure investment	– 2.5	0.0
Present value of 'productive' investment projects	15.0	11.0
Total present values	**12.5**	**11.0**

In the above case, method A shows a more realistic discount rate being used to evaluate both 'productive' and infrastructure investment to give an NPV of £12.5m. If, in method B, only the 'productive' investment is evaluated at a discount rate of 15 per cent, then the 'answer' would have become a mere £11m, which is substantially lower than the more realistic figure of £12.5m in method A.

Financial theory also suggests that a *time horizon* for estimating cash flows needs to be set. This horizon may reach up to the very end of the life of the project or, where a project's life may be particularly long or indefinite, up to that point where cash flow definition becomes increasingly uncertain. Where the forecast period is short or the project has a long life cycle, the terminal value can make up a substantial part of the NPV of the project (Copeland *et al*). Yet a temptation for managers is to spend less time exploring behind 'terminal value' as it is only a single variable amongst many in any financial modelling process, even where it is a substantial element in the NPV.

The twin curses of uncertainty and risk

A major problem arises where a number of key variables are uncertain. Financial theory offers a range of approaches for dealing with this problem including:

- The use of statistical analysis to explore the probability distribution of individual variables. These probability distributions may be superimposed to yield an overall probability distribution for the NPV of a project.
- The use of 'certainty equivalents' to generate assumptions. In this approach managers are asked what *certain* value they would swap for the opportunity given its degree of uncertainty and to be indifferent between the two options (Tomkins, 1991).[12] For example, are you indifferent between an NPV of £3m which was 50 per cent probable versus an NPV of £10m which was only 25 per cent probable?
- Sensitivity analysis to consider the impact of NPV on a change in one or more key variables

Taking each of these points in turn, statistical approaches may represent a way of dealing with risk and uncertainty, but these approaches have drawbacks, if not major headaches. For instance they are relatively complex to use and interpret (despite recent advances in computer modelling). They are most useful for what has been described as 'well structured' problems – many types of major investment decisions are less well structured and clear-cut, not only less tangible business investments but also many of the more traditional areas of 'capital investment'.

Certainty equivalents have the advantage of appearing simpler and more straightforward but these depend on identifying managers' personal 'utility functions' (which may vary considerably) trading off benefit with risk. They also hide 'low' and 'high' risks within in a single currency of 'certain cash'.

Finally, financial theory suggests that sensitivity analysis can be of great value. It should be based on assessment of *level* of risk, thereby avoiding the use of a fixed percentage change in the variable (the 'ten per cent sensitivity' analysis syndrome). Sensitivity analysis can also be performed by 'working backwards'. Here each assumption is taken in turn and tested to identify the degree of volatility which can be tolerated whilst avoiding a negative NPV.

Financial theory prescribes against increasing the discount rate to make adjustment for project-related risk. This is frowned on for two reasons. First long-term cash flows are unduly penalised due to the compounding effect, and second, because this practice rests on a confusion between project-specific risk (or risk which is inherent in the cash flows of that project) and systematic risk. 'Systematic risk' isolates the covariance of the project's returns to the stock market as a whole – the latter being seen as the total 'system' which investors are investing in. Financial theory also argues that the cost of capital (if computed using the capital asset market theory) already takes into account this 'systematic' risk and therefore to increase the discount rate for a 'risk premium' is to double count the adjustment for risk. Project-specific risk should, according to financial theory, be isolated by making realistic projections for the project rather than by adding a risk premium.

Financial theory does not, therefore, seem to resolve the problems which managers face in practice in dealing with risk and uncertainty. Kaplan described the evolution of financial tools, including discounting, in the early part of the century against a background of relative predictability and stability of external markets. In that era, managers only had to consider forecasting sales volumes, prices and costs, etc in formulating key assumptions. Although this approach may have worked well up even to the mid-twentieth century it may be inappropriate today due to increasing external change. Nevertheless, the influence of an internally orientated mind-set within financial analysis may remain strong.

Seeing into the mist – *valuing future and contingent opportunity*

Finally, a particularly difficult problem is that of valuing future opportunity which may occur as a spin-off to making the investment. Here financial theory *does* have something to say, based on 'option theory' (Brealey and Myers). This deals with the valuation of options on the securities markets. But in order to use option theory managers need to be able to judge the likely value of the opportunity, and also the likely conditions and probability of it arising. Neither of these variables are easy to arrive at.

Option theory is not put forward very convincingly by financial theory as a tool which managers can readily put into practice. But the problem of appraising future opportunity *is* a significant issue, as highlighted by Haspeslagh and Jemison (1991)[13] in evaluating acquisitions made as a 'platform' into either an adjacent or emerging industry. It is also an important issue, for example, for oil companies when a decision to invest may well be contingent on the future level of oil prices.

This overview leads to the conclusion that, from a practical point of view, existing financial theory represents at best a partial framework for decision-making. Further, the areas where it appears weakest are those which involve high levels of uncertainty, interdependency with other projects and to areas of existing business activity. These characteristics may, in the 1990s, be more the rule than the exception for investment decision-making.

Practical perils

Research studies have uncovered a number of major problems which managers face when estimating incremental cash flow.

1. Managers find it difficult to assess the 'base case' when picturing what the cash flows of the business will look like *without* the investment (Barwise *et al*). The 'base case' needs to be understood in depth before working on the 'investment case' and this may require some in depth strategic and financial analysis.
2. Hard to quantify benefits are often excluded from the project appraisal (Barwise *et al*). Again, the Cranfield cases in Chapters 5 and 6 confirmed this, but they also highlighted the importance of protecting both the credibility of a business case and that managers' concerns about the need for measurement and control inhibit the inclusion of these benefits.
3. Managers handle risk and uncertainty in a wide diversity of ways. In Pike's survey only 37 per cent used risk analysis as a financial appraisal tool. Even where sensitivity analysis is undertaken, typically involving computer spreadsheet models, in practice this activity is often used as a means of 'absorbing uncertainty'. In the Cranfield research, Post Office Counters appeared to use the most sophisticated

techniques of risk assessment although here managers were concerned about this leading (possibly) to oversophistication.

The Cranfield research illustrates that incremental analysis is not always self-evident. For instance, one manager from IDV recalls past problems in a previous industry where marginal analysis could send dangerously misleading signals to decision makers:

> I was in the toiletries industry. To lay down a machine costs £60m . . . you always filled the machine up to 50 per cent over the top and then put in a new machine . . . And you went out and you did go for more business. When you filled the machines up and over the top [of capacity], how do you justify the new equipment? Because you do have an option of getting out of the business. Therefore you should justify your machine in your *least* profitable business, and you couldn't do that.

The above example highlights vividly how the wider context of a major investment decision needs to be explored. This may involve not only the investment itself but whether the business *as a whole* is profitable, and in what circumstances.

The problems of risk assessment are highlighted by Rolls Royce in the Cranfield research:

> I think the problem is, we have two big imponderables. The market is one, the actual cost of developing the engine is the other, with the time scales and inherent technological risk. By the time you've put these two together, you've got a nonsense effectively if you try to do a statistical analysis of that.

In this particular case where managers trace back the drivers of uncertainty and risk one emerges which is hard for them to evaluate:

> There is probably a 50 per cent chance that the price of fuel will go up and a 50 per cent chance that it will go down in real terms over the next decade. How do you quantify it?

These 'practical perils' lead one to the – apparently inescapable – conclusion that techniques of financial appraisal have become too concerned with the mechanics of analysis and unconcerned with getting a handle on the root drivers of financial value.

SUMMARY AND CONCLUSIONS

The key points of this chapter can therefore be summarised as follows:

- Financial theory does not see 'the unit of analysis' as problematical.

Managers themselves appear unaware that the definition of 'the unit of analysis' may play a powerful role itself in the appraisal process.

- Typically, managers try to use a basket of financial tools for appraising major investment decisions but there remain significant ambiguities on how best to use these tools, with payback and IRR being often preferred to NPV in practice.

- 'Judgmental' and qualitative factors, in parallel with quantitative analysis, play a significant, if not major, role in practice. But managers find it difficult to bring these two different pictures of 'value' together as a single vision and may see these as fundamentally in tension.

- Managers are often uncertain about what 'cost of capital' to use, and when. Although the cost of capital *is* an issue to be grappled with, it is not the only issue and may be of lower relative importance than many others depending on the decision context.

- Managers do not appear to be comfortable relying on a single financial measure (whether IRR or NPV) to capture their total assessment of a major investment decision.

- Capital rationing and associated financial constraints (especially in meeting reported earnings targets) is a very important problem, rather than a secondary issue facing managers.

- Managers can face severe problems in defining the base case. This can occur in quantifying less tangible benefits (and costs) and also in defining the levels of risk and uncertainty surrounding the 'incremental cash flows'.

The above factors are illustrated graphically in the four core cases in Chapters 6 and 7 of this book. But standing back from these points, a key misunderstanding within prior theory and practice emerges. Financial theory may have been thought in the past as providing a necessary *and sufficient* set of frameworks for managers to deal effectively with appraisal issues. But this is questionable – other appraisal techniques, including strategic appraisal, may be necessary to provide a more complete and 'sufficient' set of tools. As a result it may be hardly surprising that managers experience difficulties in using financial tools as the *primary* method of appraisal in practice.

Financial theory may, therefore, have been oversold as being the core discipline – providing the answer to all or even most of the problems of investment appraisal. Although some appraisal problems may be due to inappropriate use of financial tools, it is suggested that strategic analysis provides the necessary ingredient required to enrich the decision process. In the next chapter, we turn to how strategic vision may achieve this objective.

REFERENCES

1. Brealey, R and Myers, S (1984) *Principles of Corporate Finance*, McGraw Hill, Maidenhead
2. King, P (1975) 'Is the emphasis of Capital Budgeting Theory Misplaced?', *Journal of Business Finance and Accounting*, vol 2, no 1, pp 69–82
3. Pike, R H and Dobbins, R (1984) *Investment Decisions and Financial Strategy*, Philip Allan, Oxford
4. Barwise, P, Marsh, P, Thomas, K and Wensley, R (1988) *Managing Strategic Investment Decisions in Large Diversified Companies*, London Business School
5. Fielding, J (1989) 'Is Beta Better?', *Management Accounting*, November, pp 38–40
6. Copeland, T, Koller, T and Murrin, J (1990) *Valuation – Measuring and Managing the Value of Companies*, John Wiley, Chichester
7. Simmonds, K (1984) *The Accounting Assessment of Competitive Position*, London Business School Paper
8. Kaplan, R S (1986) 'Must CIM be Justified by Faith Alone?', *Harvard Business Review*, pp 87-95, March-April
9. Coulthurst, N J and Sizer, J (1984) *A Casebook of British Management Accounting* vol 1, The Institute of Chartered Accountants in England and Wales
10. Kaplan, R S (1987) *Relevance Lost – The Rise and Fall of Management Accounting*, Harvard Business School Press, Boston
11. Coulthurst, N J (1986) 'The Application of the Incremental Principle in Capital Investment Project Evaluation', *Accounting and Business Research*, pp 359-364, Autumn
12. Tomkins, C (1991) *Corporate Resource Allocation – Financial, Strategic and Organisational Perspectives*, Basil Blackwell, Oxford
13. Haspeslagh, P C and Jemison, D B (1991) *Managing Acquisitions – Creating Value through Corporate Renewal*, The Free Press, Macmillan, New York

4

LINKING STRATEGY AND FINANCIAL VALUE

INTRODUCTION

This chapter explores whether strategy can alleviate many of the problems which financial theory raised in Chapter Three. This is done in a number of stages. First, we examine the strategic critique of financial theory in order to pinpoint where the errors and oversimplifications are in applying financial theory. Second, we explore approaches of 'shareholder value analysis' and associated theories of 'competitive value creation'. Finally, we integrate the ideas which are implicit in existing theory from this chapter and the previous chapters on strategic and financial theory into a 'linkage framework'. This linkage framework was used by managers from the four research sites to reflect on their problems of making major investment decisions.

THE CRITIQUE OF FINANCIAL THEORY

Strategic theorists have criticised financial theory and practice on a number of grounds:

If applied mechanistically, financial theory might have prevented some valuable investment decisions of high value (for example, Quinn, 1980, describes the grounds for investment by Pilkingtons in the float-glass process as 'visionary' – where uncertainty was so great that a positive NPV could not have been justified).[1]

The point that past visionary and successful projects would have been prevented if financial appraisal techniques had been used rigorously may suggest to us that areas of future and contingent value creation may require separate identification in the appraisal. This separating out of different kinds of value might ensure that the fuzziness of an opportunity does not preclude it being evaluated in financial terms.

The focus on incremental cash flows of projects as stand alone areas of activity, together with the prescription that projects with positive NPVs should be undertaken (except where capital rationing applies) may encourage investment to be spread too thinly. These characteristics may represent, in effect, a *financial incrementalism*. The result may be that *a)* investment needs of different business areas viewed as a whole are neglected; *b)* important positive (or even negative) synergies between businesses and specific projects are missed; and *c)* managers are encouraged to believe they are 'safe' because they have merely produced a set of self-justifying financial numbers.

Another criticism is that although financial theory tries to accommodate the trade-off between long- and short-term value through discounting, in practice managers may apply higher discount rates than are appropriate on purely theoretical grounds. This may be due to the perceived need for capital rationing, or to the felt need to correct for over-optimism in assumptions. Or, it may also be due simply to managers being unaware that their 'true' cost of capital is much lower than what they believe (Hayes and Garvin, 1982).[2]

Further, although financial incrementalism deems that managers should identify the *base case* for the investment – what happens in the business without the investment – there is a hidden implication that the base case is *steady-state*. Yet there may be a raft of reasons – competitive, regulatory, technological change and so on – which make the 'base case' either declining or perhaps more rarely, improving. As many areas of investment essentially protect the existing cash flows of the business then it is perhaps understandable that managers using 'steady-state' base case assumptions find it difficult to justify vital investment decisions using financial tools (Hayes and Garvin; Kaplan, 1986).[3]

Although financial theory emphasises the importance of 'getting the right hurdle rate', in practice this is merely one variable and one which may be *less* important in determining NPV than others.

Finally, there is criticism of the tendency towards 'manipulating the numbers' to arrive at 'the right answer' or a pre-conceived view of NPV (Quinn). In effect, this becomes a form of 'insensitivity analysis' (ie managers look for a plausible combination of variables which gives them the answer which they are looking for).

In order to evaluate these general criticisms it may be useful now to examine a number of questions:

- Do the problems highlighted by strategic theorists indicate that financial appraisal tools are inherently flawed, or is it simply a result of managers using them improperly?

- Or is strategic theory suggesting that whatever you might do to educate managers about these techniques they will inevitably bias or manipulate them in the realities of the decision-making process?
- Does this critique imply that the role of financial appraisal should be considerably curtailed in favour of evaluation through strategic and broader, qualitative criteria?

Certainly it may be more likely that in the main these problems result from the mis-application of financial tools rather than from the tools themselves. Also, it might be unwise to recoil from the apparent difficulty of linking strategic and financial appraisal simply because in the past financial appraisal appears to have been in conflict with 'strategic' criteria in practice.

Let us therefore now turn to competitive theories of value creation which might shed more light on how strategic and financial appraisal might be linked.

MANAGING FOR SHAREHOLDER VALUE

Competitive theories of value creation (shareholder value analysis, or SVA) represents an unusual blend of strategic and financial theory. SVA builds from Porter's concepts of competitive advantage (1985)[4] and seeks to integrate competitive analysis with the use of financial appraisal techniques borrowed from corporate finance. These methods were explored thoroughly in Chapter 3.

Although competitive strategy focuses at the strategic business unit, rather than the project, level, a strategic business unit (SBU) may be considered to be a quasi-project whose cash flows can be computed and which therefore has an NPV. Discounted Cash Flow (DCF) techniques can therefore be applied to an *existing* set of business projects as well as to new or incremental areas of investment. However, reappraisal of existing investment in a business using DCF appears to be a rare phenomenon. This is perhaps because managers do not wish to find out how right or wrong they have been in their past estimates of future cash flows. One area of exception in the past includes the reevaluation of a stream of past acquisitions to identify whether value has been created or lost. Another application is to reappraise corporate strategy using DCF as a means of constructing defensive or offensive strategies in takeover battles. Notably these exceptions arose not because managers *felt like* reappraisal of past decisions, but as a result of external interventions.

In addition to SBU reappraisal, shareholder value analysis can also be used to evaluate SBUs as a corporate portfolio. Besides the value a business has given its current ownership, it is also feasible to assess what it might be worth in broad terms to another owner who may be able to harvest new synergies or eradicate areas of value lost. But even the application of basic shareholder value theory requires some basic refocusing of attitude which is elucidated by a Rolls Royce manager:

> It seems to me that the things we are probably going to have to do in education within our companies is that the money goes out of the door, it is a cash item irrespective of whether it is capital, revenue or anything else . . . what you are investing in is your future.

Although on the surface this may appear to be a simple change in thinking, it may have a major impact in shifting attitudes on:

1. the financial appraisal of non-capital areas of investment, including brands, image, and collaborative arrangements;
2. the use of DCF to appraise expenditure normally defined as 'revenue' but having long-term benefits – eg within reorganisations, management development programmes, quality initiatives, and even efforts to shift culture and management style.
3. the use of financial tools to reappraise *existing* businesses to highlight where value is being created or dissipated: this can even extend to valuing the impact of Head Office. The latter may raise some direct and perhaps embarrassing questions on where, whether and how much value a Head Office adds (or even possibly destroys).

The above list of 'target areas' may present difficulties not merely of an analytical nature (which can be very difficult – eg when managers are trying to put a value on less tangible areas such as 'culture change' or quality programmes) but also in adjusting the management process. They involve major extensions of the role of valuation from the realm of tangible, capital projects to both capital and non-capital and to some areas of revenue costs. This is as well as (probably) a shift from an accounting basis of measurement to an economic one. Chapter 8, the case of BP, further highlights the scale of the task involved in applying shareholder value analysis, but equally pinpoints some major benefits.

Exponents of shareholder value analysis (SVA)

Turning now to the nuts and bolts of this approach, the primary exponent of SVA is Alfred Rappaport in the US (1986).[5] He has now been rapidly followed by others (Reimann, 1990;[6] Copeland, Koller and Murrin, 1990[7]). Rappaport's contribution to thinking includes:

- The insight that Porter's five forces, generic strategies and the idea of a 'value-chain' can be linked directly to the key cash generators in a business – its value- and cost-drivers.
- Typically, a relatively small number of value- and cost-drivers account for the value and volatility of the NPV of either a business or a new investment project, for example levels of margin are closely related to competitive rivalry.
- Furthermore, the cost of capital is merely one variable which drives value. Frequently the measurement error associated with this variable is much smaller than that of the external, competitive variables (Reimann).
- Competitive analysis might thus embrace not merely qualitative factors including market attractiveness and competitive position, but also the evaluation of the ensuing stream of cash flows. Computing the NPV of different strategic options and also for different SBUs might therefore form an important tool for strategy formulation – at both business and corporate levels.

On the first two points above, it might be useful to illustrate what 'cost' and 'value' drivers are. For instance, in a recent advisory project which I undertook for a high technology business, key cost drivers were identified as:

- complexity of product and service range;
- the negotiated price of bought-in technical supplies;
- under-utilised capacity;
- management style and systems – these generated additional costs through inadequate filtering of new opportunity and through producing an unbalanced allocation of internal skills to key projects.

The above example also highlights that underlying cost drivers can represent a quite different cut of the 'cost cake' from conventional accounting records.

Value-drivers require equally in-depth assessment. For example, in the earlier case of Stratech (Chapter 2) in-depth interviews with customers revealed that:

- major existing customers did not see it as important that Stratech was 'international' nor that it had a particularly reputable holding company;
- on the other hand, some customers actually disliked Stratech's fairly

aggressive approach to winning business – a feature which lost rather than won a lot of business.

- whilst Stratech itself felt that having a prominent site near London was expensive and perhaps unnecessary, customers *did* perceive this as important and that it added stature and credibility to the company.

Clearly it is not possible to say mechanistically that each of the above features taken independently added or subtracted £X to shareholder value. But what is evident is that *taken as a whole* a quantum level shift in perceived image might have allowed Stratech to advance sales by approximately Y per cent and margin by approximately Z per cent.

Coming back now to the various 'flavours' of SVA on offer, the two main approaches are from *a)* Reimann and *b)* Copeland *et al.*

Reimann, although a keen exponent of SVA, is cautious about overuse of financial appraisal, warning that managers should be sensitive and alert to the quality and soundness of their underlying assumptions. Rappaport appears to share similar concerns. Both stress (in varying degrees) that financial vision must be lit by strategic insight.

Copeland *et al* place far more emphasis on the sophistication of financial analysis rather than on the importance of surfacing and analysing competitive sources of uncertainty. Although Copeland's book contains some useful contributions to the debate – including the weighted average estimation of cost of capital for divisions of a conglomerate – it does seem to be still very much in the tradition of prescribing sophisticated financial theory as the prime treatment for the condition. By contrast, Reimann gives perhaps a simpler and more practical account of the opportunities and problems of implementing SVA-type approaches.

Benefits of SVA

SVA gives us a number of useful insights into linkages between strategic and financial appraisal. It can help identify some key areas where competitive variables drive financial variables. This can provide a more complete 'picture' of the overall 'system' or context of which the investment (or business) is a part, ie the 'business system'. SVA also encourages managers to question the basis for any positive NPV, for instance, how does the supposed attractiveness (of the opportunity) exploit specific market imperfections? How is the firm uniquely placed either to create or exploit imperfections? How long and how sustainable is both *a)* the apparent attractiveness and *b)* competitive position?

If positive answers cannot be found to these three questions then the basis for a NPV is, at best, dubious.

Key areas where financial value can be subjected to detailed competitive and outward-looking tests thus include the following:

- Applying DCF to evaluate the corporate portfolio and not merely at project level. Rolls Royce Aeroengines managers take this idea up explicitly in Chapter 6, followed by Post Office Counters Limited in Chapter 7.
- Providing financial tools to test any claims that 'synergy' exists – otherwise this might be left as a dangerously vague idea (Rappaport).
- By suggesting that we need to explore the *terminal value* of a business at the end of a particular time horizon (say five or more years out). This might encourage managers to generate more insight into the future than if they were simply to paint a broad scenario. More in depth probing of the underlying competitive position at the end of the period of 'foreseeability' might thus clarify what would otherwise be an ill-disciplined vision.
- By raising the issue of 'value-capture' – ie the extent to which value is created by an investment captured by the company or by the customer depending upon the patterns of competitive pressure and sustainability of a position (Ghemawat, 1991).[8] For illustration, Stratech might succeed in shifting its image but then find it hard to encash the increase in perceived value margins by improving margins – because of buyers' high negotiating power. The value might thus be harvested purely through expanding sales volumes.
- Finally, SVA helps to dislodge, if not dissolve, the myth that strategic and financial theory are inevitably at loggerheads.

Indeed, partly as a consequence of being involved in the Cranfield research, the corporate planning manager at Rolls Royce experimented with valuing business strategies and in examining the contribution of individual projects to that value (see Chapter 6). This generated some important insights for Rolls Royce into where the main value was being generated by existing business and major project strategies. Without using an SVA approach, it is very unlikely that these insights would have arisen (see also Chapter 8 on BP.)

One Rolls Royce manager highlights for us the attractions of SVA as a guiding concept:

> People may ask, why are you doing all of this discounting? – the concept, I suppose. A general understanding of why you need to deliver an IRR of Y per cent, because it is related to the cost of capital in servicing shareholder value. That connection is really not well made.
>
> I like the concept of valuing a bit of business, not just a project. I mean a

whole operating unit and say, what's the kind of strategy we are into, what is it worth?

Prior to the Cranfield research, Post Office Counters Limited had also experimented with similar approaches (although these were not explicitly called 'SVA'):

> Additionally, however, is the assessment of the non-financials. Last year we looked at various categories which the answers were 'yes' or 'no' to; such as the quality of service, allocating point scores which were slightly notional. We allocated 20,000 per point and added these up to arrive at notional NPVs for all projects. This year the corporate people are developing something called 'goal programming techniques' based on linear programming.

The above shift at Post Office Counters involved taking the decision process into new and unfamiliar territory – as we will see in parallel within the BP case (Chapter 8).

This change process may involve an early phase of scepticism and hesitation until some practical results are yielded. The following case study of a process-intensive company will help to illustrate this point.

Short case study – Techtron

A process-intensive company, which we will call Techtron, sought to 'map' the value of a number of major R&D projects. Techtron's objective was to link the strategic and financial assumptions underlying these projects. Techtron managers found it invaluable to use a matrix (see Figure 4.1).

The axes of Techtron's matrix were relatively simple – 'return' was plotted as both the IRR (vertical axis) and as NPV. The NPV was depicted in proportion to the size of the circles (the circle shaded black represents a negative NPV).

After the matrix was plotted a number of strategic questions then arose. The managers discovered that many of their less attractive projects were ones which demanded a higher level of ongoing spend in order to comply with regulatory standards.

Also, the 'risk' dimension enabled Techtron's managers to begin to disaggregate risk so that it could be understood in its more basic components. In this example these included market and competitive risk, regulatory risk, and operational risk (or those risks associated with 'will it work?'). Interestingly, *regulatory* risk appeared to be the most important factor driving value and was also an area where products diverged

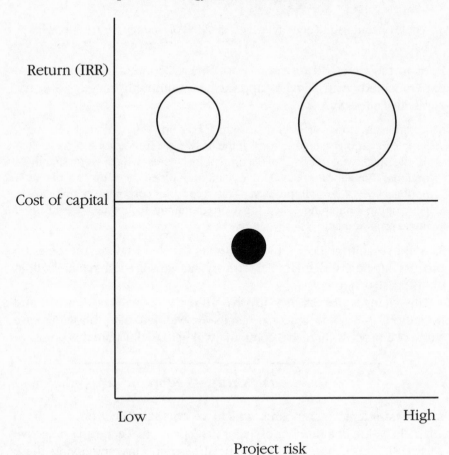

Figure 4.1 Techtron's R & D appraisal matrix

considerably. A separate matrix was drawn up purely to plot this kind of risk against return.

This analysis thus raised some major questions about the robustness of cash flows of certain projects. Sensitivity analysis could be then focused primarily on exploring the areas of greatest vulnerability.

In the above example, managers appeared taken aback when the full power of pictorial tools to display and compare both *quantitative* and *qualitative* variables was revealed. This led to some challenging questions about whether the existing pattern of resource allocation was appropriate within Techtron.

SVA approaches may, however, suffer a number of major general disadvantages. First, there are technical and analytical issues which may prove difficult to unravel. For example, there is the problem of estimating terminal values (according to the experience of BP, the percentage of present value contained within the terminal value can be over 50 per cent of NPV). The terminal value can obscure both over-optimism and under-optimism in valuing a business or project opportunity. For example, they might fail to capture the probability that a stream of cash flows may go into decline due to a *future* change in the industry structure or due simply to obsolescence and a loss of competitive advantage. Equally, they may omit the value of future opportunities which are likely to spin off. Maybe managers are content to believe that this is a 'swings and roundabouts' situation but that it is highly likely that some investment avenues are more likely to end as cul-de-sacs than others.

Second, SVA approaches do not in themselves resolve how managers make fundamental judgements on the uncertain competitive variables which drive value. For this we need to look elsewhere to ways in which managers can surface and compare the key assumptions which underly the eventual business case – this involves dealing with decision process issues more than technical analysis.

Third, SVA approaches can take many years to bed down – according to one BP manager who was involved extensively in the SVA initiative at BP from the mid- to late-80s it has taken nearly five years to 'spread the message that business strategies should be financially evaluated using DCF-based methods'.

Apart from these difficulties, SVA approaches share some limitations with those strategic and financial theories already discussed. First, SVA can become prescriptive and runs a major risk of being a 'management fad' (various brands have been – 'shareholder value analysis' – Rappaport; 'value-based planning' or 'value-based strategic management' – Reimann). If any term is to be used, the writer's own preference is for 'strategic value management' or 'SVM' to stress that both strategic vision and value appraisal play *equal and balancing* roles.

Second, in addition to the already severe prescriptive burdens placed on managers by both financial and strategic theory, SVA approaches may entail imposing yet another layer of 'must do's'. (For instance, Copeland *et al*'s book might be daunting even to a financial director with strategic management training and who has been exposed to advanced corporate finance theory.)

Third the published material on SVA does not appear to address how these tools might fit within the management process. We know from research on strategic decision-making (see the next chapter) that this process is complex, unpredictable and highly intuitive – not the highly structured and rational process which may be required for SVA approaches to bolt onto easily. The latter part of this book focuses on the practical opportunities for and difficulties in achieving significant shift in decision processes. It does not duck the question of 'what is the value of value management?' Following recent contact by the writer with a number of corporate planners in major organisations, many managers appear drawn to SVA because it promises moving beyond the financially-based earnings measures, but are then daunted by the potential difficulty of implementing the change involved. These difficulties involve not only 'when, where and how to begin', but also involve selling the idea to both top management in a group and to front-line operational managers that there is obvious 'value' in 'value management'.

Fourth, there is also a major problem of ex-post measuring and comparing estimated cash flows against realised cash flows. This is particularly relevant to specific projects whose incremental effect on the business is fuzzy or where there has been major change in the definition of the business. The latter may occur, for example, through restructuring, through acquisitions or through major organic development.

Fifth, in its published forms, SVA appears to play down the difficulties of extrapolating projections beyond the time horizon over which managers can meaningfully picture the future. Recent thinking by Ghemawat emphasises the need for managers to 'slice the future' into discrete but progressive periods of increasing uncertainty. This might involve, for example, looking at the next two years applying 'current' competitive conditions, the following two years with some specific trends researched in detail and the final four years as a broad scenario. But Ghemawat certainly does not downplay the difficulty of what is, in effect, 'seeing over the horizon'. The longer the time horizon is, the more this uncertainty becomes compounded. Also, interdependencies between uncertain variables become increasingly difficult to anticipate, resulting in nonlinear interaction between variables and 'very complicated structures' (Ghemawat) and hence to the earlier mentioned 'curse' of uncertainty.

Finally, SVA does not appear to address how to set about unravelling interdependencies. For example, Ghemawat emphasises that 'flexibility' has an inherent value; that a group of activities may be indivisible and thus not amenable to simple, incremental analysis; and also that inter-dependencies between discrete product/market strategies can play a major role in value creation.

We might, therefore, be tempted to conclude that SVA may suffer the same fate that financial, project-related approaches have already run: managers may fail to apply techniques properly because of a variety of learning, behavioural and organisational constraints. The idea of SVA may fall into disrepute because it may be oversold and also because managers may believe that it is simple to 'plug it into' existing management processes without realising the scale of change involved. In my own view this would be a great pity as many of the ideas of SVA (if made readily operational) can be used to fundamentally reshape the strategic and financial decision-making and control process.

The key insights which we can draw from SVA are therefore as follows:

- In many cases the 'unit of analysis' should be made higher up the hierarchy of business investment – it may be a set of projects, a specific area of the business or even the business itself.
- The *principal* and most important linkages between strategic and financial appraisal may be simplified through analysis of key value and cost drivers.
- Managers may be able to assign financial value to all, or the majority, of the perceived *strategic value* of an investment decision, providing they do not seek to be one hundred per cent accurate.
- Applying DCF- and financially-based analysis to a particular investment strategy might be used to encourage rather than discourage the tendency to longer-term thinking.
- The strategic assumptions underlying terminal value require thorough exploration.
- Finally, financial analysis may be used to sharpen up what would otherwise be unclear strategic thinking; likewise strategic thinking might generate more vision and insight than would be feasible through relying upon financial appraisal alone. A potential area for breakthrough here is the use of strategic appraisal grids alongside financial measures to show 'NPV' and other measures against a competitive context (see Chapter 2, Figure 2.2). This approach represents a genuine evolution of thinking away from the idea that in practice NPV means only that 'numbers prevent vision'.

A FRAMEWORK FOR LINKING STRATEGIC AND FINANCIAL APPRAISAL FOR LONGER-TERM FINANCIAL DECISIONS

Overview

The linkage framework is now set out partly as pictures and partly in words, and has four main ingredients:

1. When is a longer-term financial decision strategic?
2. Types of appraisal problems
3. Linkages between strategic and financial appraisal
4. Stages and outputs of decision-making.

First, how can managers identify those areas of longer-term financial decisions which are *strategic* from those which are more *tactical?* Although inevitably there will be some areas which are borderline, a useful way of distinguishing financial decisions with strategic impact is through asking whether that decision involves a change in competitive style or scope ('what business are we in' and 'with what focus'); is simply large in relation to the business, or a combination of all these.

The idea of 'competitive style' was derived from Porter's concept of generic strategies to denote whether a differentiation or cost leadership strategy was in place. It was believed that the word 'style' had more fit with the understanding of UK managers than the word 'generic'. These criteria can be depicted as in Figure 4.2.

In Figure 4.2 financial decision A is in minor replacement plant and involves no real shift of competitive scope and style. It does not involve substantial investment, therefore on all three counts it looks more like a 'tactical' investment.

By contrast, financial decision B involves replacement of a facility with newer technology, thus involving a change in the competitive base of the company (and thus its style). It also involves more substantial investment. Although it does not involve extending competitive scope it appears to be more of a 'strategic' than a 'tactical' investment. To illustrate B-type projects, a food business was considering replacement of a specialist production line for one particular product line. The investment ran into several millions of pounds yet the analysis of its likely value was based on internally-focused assumptions, assuming that the 'market' would be stable. It was not until late in the day that managers raised the question as to whether this stability could be assumed and whether the brand might be subject to competitive erosion.

Finally, investment C involved a shift into a new area of activity (competitive scope) *and* a shift in competitive style. Although the perceived investment itself was not very large, it could be argued that on the first two counts it merited the description 'strategic'. To illustrate, certain of Stratech's new products fell into this category – involving penetration of new market segments, the use of newer technology *and* a strategy of differentiation (as opposed to cost leadership).

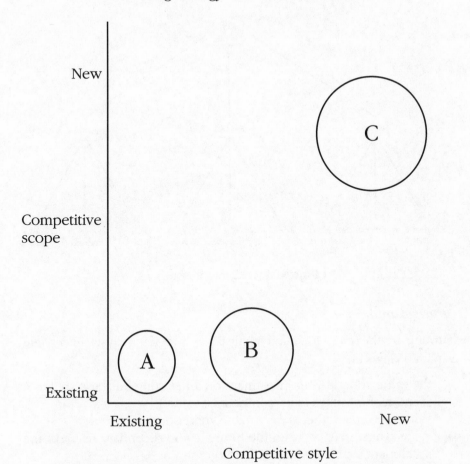

Figure 4.2 When is a longer-term financial decision 'strategic'

Key content issues

In order to analyse the key problems involved in the appraisal it is helpful first to distinguish the content-related issues from those to do with process. First, Figure 4.3 describes the key areas of content issues.

Following Barwise *et al* (1988), the key content issues are split between strategic, financial and operational. The Cranfield research suggested not only that managers often compartmentalise strategic and financial appraisal but also that operational appraisal itself may become fragmented away from the other two areas. Managers may assume that a project which has 'strategic fit' and is 'financially attractive' can be implemented when this may not be the case.

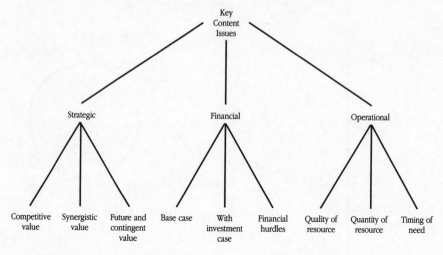

Figure 4.3 Content issues

Strategic analysis

Turning to the more detailed analysis, 'strategic' analysis may yield separate views on:

- the value added by an investment on an existing business area as a 'stand-alone' entity (or its 'competitive value');
- value created in other areas (or its 'synergistic value');
- value which may occur in the future as the secondary result of the investment (or its 'future and contingent value').

Value-adding characteristics can be diagnosed by the grid in Figure 4.4. This highlights that the zone of contingent value can be further subdivided into that which can be pinpointed to a specific business area versus that which may affect a number of business areas. For example, a small acquisition in an emerging industry may generate contingent (1) value in the form of a 'platform' for the future. But it may also generate a more current, competitive value (through acquisition of an existing, though small, competitive position).

But the development of a brand new technology may not only add to business activities directly but also may add to volume, margins, or reduce costs in existing but other areas of the business rather than those involving the particular project (ie – the contingent (2) zone).

This value grid provides a means of recognising that investment programmes are often far from homogeneous. It may also help avoid the bewilderment of financial managers who may otherwise try to evaluate

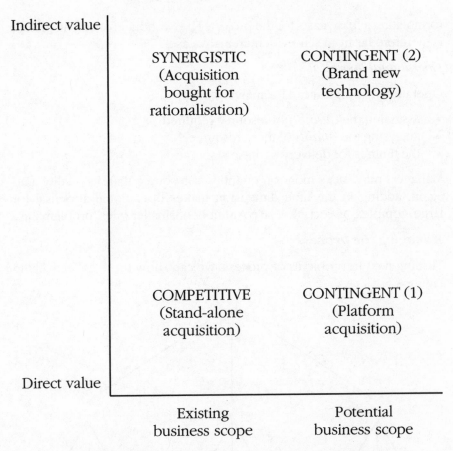

Figure 4.4 Strategic value grid (with examples)

both contingent (1) and contingent (2) areas using very precise financial measures. It is also put forward to ensure that the 'strategic' label is not applied in a cavalier way to areas of favoured investment so that decisions can avoid detailed financial probing.

Financial appraisal

This may cover:

- the analysis of the 'base' or 'without investment' case;
- comparison with the 'with investment case' to identify incremental cash flows;
- evaluation through the use of financial measures or hurdles.

As previous thinkers have highlighted, there are major problems with formulating a 'base case' for the project. The 'without investment' picture is therefore far from self-evident in many cases.

Operational appraisal

Operational appraisal can be analysed into:

- assessing the *quantity* of resource required;
- analysing the *quality* of these resources;
- the timings for delivery of these resources.

Managers may focus more on quantity of resource than its quality, and again, adding in the time dimension makes operational appraisal for large, complex projects or a large number of smaller ones, problematic.

Managing the process

Turning next to problems of process, we can show these collectively in Figure 4.5:

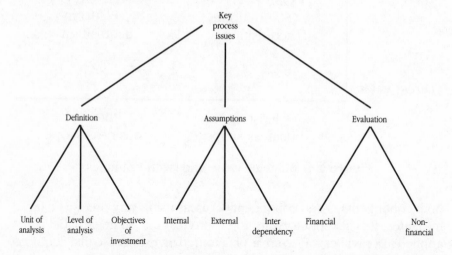

Figure 4.5 Managing the process – key issues

First, issues surrounding the definition of the financial decision include:

- What is the *unit* of analysis? This may involve, for example, gathering together a cluster of smaller projects (or a 'strategic project set') for analysis. Or it may involve breaking down a 'project' into sub-units of analysis. Finally, it may well involve generating alternative options.
- What is the *level* of analysis? This is linked to the first point on unit of analysis, and could be at the project (or group of projects) level, at the

business (or as a cluster of businesses) level, or even be taken at the corporate level (as in fully-fledged shareholder value analysis to evaluate the corporate portfolio in totality).

- Finally, what are the objectives of the financial decision? These objectives may involve generating new sources of revenue, adding to existing revenues, or reducing cost – forming its 'tangible' objectives. But equally, there may be less tangible but nevertheless key objectives. These may generate value indirectly – for example programmes to shift perceptions of corporate or business image, or to improve service quality.

Next we turn to the assumptions which are distinguished in Figure 4.5 between internal and external assumptions and interdependencies. Internal assumptions include cost savings, capacity increments, product characteristics. External assumptions include relative market share, channel and customer penetration, competitive response, economic, political and regulatory environment. Interdependencies may involve interaction of internal interdependencies (eg level of capacity utilisation will impact on unit cost levels). It will also involve interaction of external interdependencies (eg rapid market growth in the near future may attract entry by new competitors. This may subsequently lead to a price war especially if market conditions are affected by a recession now.)

The formulation of a balanced and realistic set of assumptions is at the very heart of our problem of linking strategic and financial appraisal. The tool in Figure 4.6 can be used to show each quadrant in proportion to the amount of effort spent on probing these areas of assumptions. The underlying idea behind Figure 4.6 is that an ideal profile should show no overriding dominance by any single (or pair of) area of assumptions, particularly those which are internally orientated (on the left-hand side).

This tool has been used in a number of advisory projects to explore the assumptions underlying key long-term financial decisions. During these sessions managers typically revealed that they would see over eighty per cent of the weight of analysis as being related to a combination of financial and operational and resource-related assumptions (the left-hand side). This is opposed to less than twenty per cent being related to 'competitive' or 'environmental' assumptions (the right-hand side).

Finally, in the evaluation of assumptions, it is typical to find differences in views between managers as to whether all or merely a part of the value should be financially quantified. Many financial managers, for instance, appear to lean towards the idea that all value *must* be quantified, yet at the same time recoil from valuing less tangible areas of value. However, it may be inappropriate to prescribe that all areas of value should be

Financial	Environmental
Operational Resources	Competitive

Figure 4.6 Evaluating the balance of assumptions

quantified, as this cannot take into account the varying context and types of investment facing a single business, or the variance in appraisal styles. This appraisal style appears to be considerably different across companies reflecting differences in control culture.

Linkages between strategic and financial appraisal

Value and cost drivers can be identified by drawing pictures of interrelationships (effectively a visual representation of Rappaport, 1987).[10] Figure 4.7 illustrates how these can be used to help managers begin to expand their vision of the key value and cost drivers. An important motivator may be the understanding of the strategic intent and likely investment plans and implementation capability of key players such as customers, suppliers and competitors. Competitor understanding is likely to be a key ingredient in the assessment of the likely financial impact of a strategic investment decision.

A series of matrices can be drawn which take a closer-up view of the impact on a company's internal value chain (Table 4.1). These provide checklists for identifying the internal impact of the decision on areas where value is generated directly, and also for less obvious areas where it might add value indirectly (for example through reducing the customer's costs and risks enabling prices to be increased slightly or discounting avoided).

Finally, an outcome matrix can be used to relate different financial outcomes against different external environments or 'states of the world' (Table 4.2).

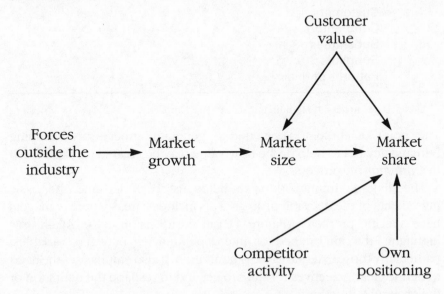

Figure 4.7 Example of value drivers

Table 4.1 Impact of investment on own value chain – checklist

Output price
Output volume
Process cost
Input cost
Input volume
Support volume and cost

Table 4.2   Matrix of outcomes and states of the world

We do:	Option A	Option B
Likely reaction:		
Customers	***	
Competitors		**
Substitutes	*	
Suppliers	*	***
Patterns of rivalry	**	

Key: * Low impact   ** Medium impact   *** High impact

The point of these tools is not to generate unnecessary planning bureaucracy but to help probe how value may be created (or destroyed) in a *questioning* process.

The 'linkage framework' also helps us to understand the basic ingredients of the decision process. This includes areas where managers have specific problems (Figure 4.8) in the decision cycle. Again, this highlights the importance of interdependencies between variables, particularly those external to the organisation. It also emphasises the need to define clear objectives for the project and to reshape the definition of the project by iteration.

Figure 4.9 (derived from Mitroff and Emshoff, 1979)[11] also helps to map assumptions by depicting their degree of (financial) impact and the degree of underlying uncertainty to address the major problem of how managers can focus on the *most critical* assumptions. For instance, during an appraisal assumption dealing with unit cost levels, A1 may change to A2 – as more data is collected certainty rises and also the impact is also perceived to be reduced. However, the shift of B1 to B2 during the same appraisal reveals increasing uncertainty and the greater impact of the assumption. This can occur, for example, as competitor entry is seen as an increasingly dangerous threat.

Table 4.3 helps to compare and prioritise projects. This involves bringing together strategic, operational and financial measures in one output for a group of projects. This table is used to understand how value is being created and can be taken through to allocating NPV to different types of value-adding activity. This helps to avoid the problem of reliance on a single figure which effectively 'collapses' a rich set of strategic and operational assumptions into a single financial figure, thereby removing insight.

Finally, Table 4.4 is a possible summary of the content of a 'business

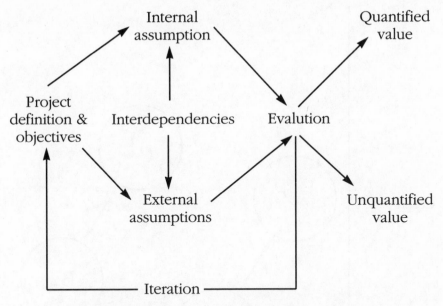

Figure 4.8 The appraisal process – an overview

case', enabling the full appraisal to be set out succinctly and in a way which raises rather than hides overall vision, both strategically and financially.

Table 4.3 Schematic comparing projects

	Project A	*Project B*
Strategic value:		
– Competitive	£x	£a
– Synergistic	£y	£b
– Opportunistic	£z	£c
Financial:		
– NPV	£p	£q
– IRR	s%	t%
– Cash distribution	cd_1	cd2
Operational:		
– Resource quantity	r_1	r2
– Resource quality	r3	r4
– Impact of timings	t_1	t2

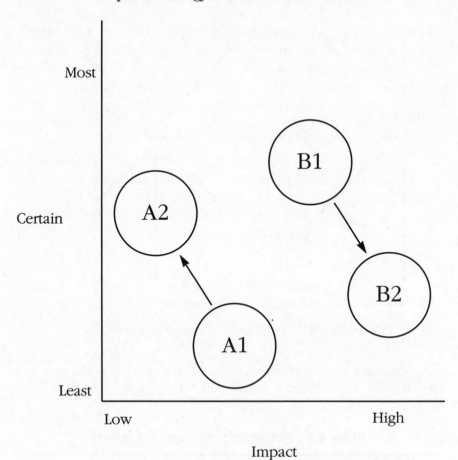

Figure 4.9 Evaluation of key assumptions

Table 4.4 Possible headings for a business case

MANAGEMENT SUMMARY	objectives, rationale, risks
DEFINITION AND SCOPE	strategic, financial, operational
OPTIONS	current and future
ASSUMPTIONS	external and internal, key interdependencies, analysis of key assumptions relating degree of uncertainty and potential financial impact
IMPLEMENTATION AND CONTINGENCY PLANS	
EVALUATION	financial and residual non-financial factors

CONCLUSION

We will return to these tools again in Chapter 10 when reviewing the implications for both practice and theory. Managers should see this broad framework as merely a starting point for tailoring their own approaches, as these tools and the checklists in Appendix 2 require close tailoring to the specific context.

Nevertheless, this framework shows that there are ways in which, in one manager's words, you can begin to 'get your arms around the problem'. There are indeed alternatives to managing longer-term financial decisions, either through financial myopia or through strategic long-sight. But let us look next at the perils inherent in the decision process itself.

REFERENCES

1. Quinn, J B (1980) *Strategies for Change – Logical Incrementalism*, Richard D Irwin, Illinois
2. Hayes, R H and Garvin, D A (1982) 'Managing as if Tomorrow Mattered', *Harvard Business Review*, pp 70–9, May–June
3. Kaplan, R S (1986) 'Must CIM be Justified by Faith Alone?', *Harvard Business Review*, pp 87–95, March–April
4. Porter, M E (1985) *Competitive Advantage*, The Free Press, New York
5. Rappaport, A (1986) *Creating Shareholder Value: The New Standard for Business Performance*, The Free Press, New York
6. Reimann, B (1990) *Managing for Value: A Guide to Value-Based Strategic Management*, Basil Blackwell, Oxford
7. Copeland, T, Koller, T and Murrin, J (1990) *Valuation – Measuring and Managing the Value of Companies*, John Wiley, Chichester
8. Ghemawat, P (1991) *Commitment, the Dynamic of Strategy*, The Free Press, Macmillan, New York
9. Barwise, P, Marsh, P, Thomas, K and Wensley, R (1988) *Managing Strategic Investment Decisions in Large Diversified Companies*, London Business School
10. Rappaport, A (1987) 'Linking Competitive Strategy and Shareholder Value Analysis', *The Journal of Business Strategy*, vol 7, no. 4, pp 58–67, Spring
11. Mitroff, I I and Emshoff, J R (1979) 'On Strategic Assumption Making: A Dialectical Approach to Policy and Planning', *Academy of Management Review*, vol 4, no 1, pp 1–12

5

LONGER-TERM FINANCIAL DECISIONS AND THE MANAGEMENT PROCESS

INTRODUCTION

This short chapter moves on to look at what is known about how decision-making processes impact on the making of major investment decisions. This is done in two stages: first the perils of incrementalism and fragmentation within the decision process are explored. A short case study follows which illustrates this in practice, followed by some general conclusions on the management process.

PERILS OF INCREMENTALISM

To begin with, there is a wealth of research in organisational theory covering the making of major business decisions which involve some implicit financial commitment. This is now illustrated by examples picked from the four core cases (which are studied in greater detail in Chapters 6 and 7), as follows:

- Strategic decisions are often made in an incremental fashion, rather than with regard to the whole of a business or to the corporate strategy (Quinn, 1980).[1] One manager illustrates this:

  We don't do an overall model of the industry to see what's happening out there when we try to justify a project targeted at a particular market. Maybe you can't do that, maybe it just produces another layer of subjectivity.

- There are recognisable stages or phases in the decision cycle. These stages are characterised, not merely by analytical activity, but also by the phenomenon of 'escalated commitment to action'. The more effort and resources are expended in an activity the more commitment builds – this is particularly relevant to the making of strategic decisions. Yet many managers are perhaps unaware just how quickly commitment snowballs. This phenomenon highlights the importance of top manager input to ideas at an early stage of idea generation and preliminary evaluation in order to help shape strategic objectives for a project, to consider other options and to define its scope and limitations.

- Ghemawat (1991)[2] also identifies the importance of assessing what he calls the 'learn-to-burn' rate in making and implementing strategic decisions. Depending on the decision context and managers' learning capability both as individuals and as teams, managers' rate of learning about an opportunity may be much slower than the build-up of commitment. This can be a particular problem for companies which are able to grow very quickly in core activities but then begin unwise diversification; it is also highly relevant to the group which is set on a growth path through a rapid series of acquisitions.
- Decisions may pass through or be affected by a multitude of decision subsystems within an organisation. They can therefore be accelerated, delayed or recycled rather than proceed in a homogeneous and linear way. In some cases the process can take not merely months, but indeed years to bring to fruition.
- Information is filtered a number of times during the decision-making process. Managers use these filters to simplify (and sometimes to oversimplify) the nature of the problem or opportunity, possibly leading to a dangerous in-group myopia or 'group think'. This phenomenon has major implications for understanding decision processes involved in evaluating complex investment decisions. The capacity of individuals and the wider organisation to analyse 'the problem' or 'opportunity' may appear to be at full stretch in coping with this degree of complexity. Again, one manager states:

> We have used scenarios . . . we have had 'highs' and 'lows'. Our tendency was to shoot for the one in the middle. It somewhat devalued the process and we don't do that any longer . . . we didn't feel that we wanted to put more and more numbers or lines on pictures that made it look even more complex and confusing.

The cases in Chapters 6 and 7 also reveal a number of other important factors of the decision process. The first is that financial modelling provides a vehicle for greatly extending the power of financial appraisal. This can, however, have drawbacks. One manager explains:

Finance are the people who could impact on the decision quite dramatically through their analysis. For acquisitions, the financial people build the models although the MD will say, yes, I agree with the assumptions.

I think we try to do things, I think we try to be too clever [about getting assumptions accurate]. I don't know how you get the right balance because at the end you are expected to test your actuals against your assumptions.

But there is a danger that the softer, judgmental elements in the decision process become buried in the process of detailed modelling. Another manager says 'It is the accountants who believe the assumptions rather than worrying about the processing . . . around the assumptions there is a tremendous amount of subjectivity.'

Before we focus on these points, it is worthwhile noting that again the picture which emerges is that of decision-making as a messy and frequently tortuous process. This may involve an initial process of problem awareness moving gradually into problem diagnosis, which may be unfinished and then is put aside whilst other issues capture management's attention. After some time the decision process may then become suddenly accelerated either due to the personal influence of a particular senior executive; the short shelf-life of an opportunity (for example an acquisition or a joint venture); or simply due to a trigger which puts the idea back onto management's core agenda. But in many instances the process of making a major decision may be slow – major financial decisions move through a varying, but sometimes lengthy, gestation and evaluation cycle.

INCREMENTAL THINKING IN DEFINING MAJOR STRATEGIC OPPORTUNITIES

This has already been touched on and is now worth returning to in depth. Quinn suggested that, typically, major strategic decisions are *not* made in a holistic way, but are more frequently evaluated in relative isolation from one another (he calls this 'logical incrementalism').

This line of thought is also echoed by Mintzberg (1987)[3] who suggests that strategies emerge typically as a 'pattern in a stream of decisions' rather than as a deliberately and comprehensively articulated strategic vision. Mintzberg also suggests that companies often shift their strategic direction gradually through making ongoing incremental decisions – strategic change is thus more likely to be evolutionary rather than revolutionary. Further, strategic decisions may not be implemented in the manner which was intended in their original strategic aspirations. The typical result may be that their *realised* strategy departs materially from their *intended* strategy.

In that case, what role do *strategic decisions*, particularly those involving significant investment, play in the formulation of strategy? Some thinkers (eg Horovitz, 1984)[4] have argued that strategic decisions actually form the core building-blocks of strategy. For this school of thought, strategic thinking is *not* seen therefore as being primarily driven by an all-embracing planning process which wraps around the entire business, but by the rolling process of making incremental strategic (and equally financial) moves.

First of all, however, it may be necessary to define what one means by 'strategic' – this is far from clear to many managers. For example, one manager in the Cranfield research reflects:

> We can argue anything on strategic grounds and in our hearts think that we will make money out of it. This seems we are kidding ourselves if that is really what we mean by a strategic move. I am very cautious of this word 'strategy', but I agree that that will have to improve or enhance our position even though on the numbers today we can't actually see our way through it.

Strategic *investment* decisions appear to be a very important sub-set of strategic decisions. It could therefore be argued, following Horovitz (1984), that these major investment decisions also form the major building-blocks of strategy. Ghemawat (1991) also highlighted the importance of major investment decisions as a vehicle for crystallising the commitment to a strategy. 'Commitment' here is therefore placed at the core of the strategic management process and achieves its embodiment in financial decisions (whether 'capital' or 'non-capital') with longer-term impact.

If decisions of a non-capital nature which involve major time lags between cash outlay and inflow are included, it does seem highly plausible that business strategy is created, generally, in unison with longer-term financial decisions. For example, both product development and investment in major business restructuring involve significant time lags and substantial financial outlay and therefore are 'longer-term financial decisions' in our sense. This is notwithstanding that they have not been called conventional 'capital' investment.

The issue of what is seen by managers as 'investment' is an additional important factor influencing how managers apply both strategic and financial appraisal to long-term financial decisions. If a particular strategic programme is *not* seen as 'investment', then the chances are that it will not be exposed to DCF-based analysis and also that it may not therefore be evaluated through 'strategic' or 'competitive' analysis either.

In Chapters 6 and 7, major investment decisions *do* appear to play a role in the strategy implementation process and also, to varying degrees, in strategy formulation. A major part of these decisions are also ones which are not regarded as 'capital' – for example brand development, building technology capability, and improving business or corporate image. It would seem that in 'investment' the neat distinction made by management theory between the 'content' issues revolving around decision-making, and 'process' – in this case planning and control – blurs greatly in practice. This is certainly how managers in these two chapters saw it and perhaps because of this we should begin to understand more about why these are so intertwined, and if so, how managers can then seek to unravel issues at the root of the appraisal problem.

Some help is available here from examining past analyses of the typical stages in the decision process. According to King (1975),[5] these stages can be distinguished as follows:

- Triggering
- Screening
- Definition
- Evaluation
- Transmission
- Decision

King concluded that:

1. managers do not spend much time and effort on certain earlier critical stages (particularly during screening and definition);
2. it is often difficult to pin-point when a decision actually 'happened' as it may more frequently crystallise gradually over time;
3. again, there is often a pronounced tendency for commitment to escalate rapidly during the decision process.

Besides the importance of stages in the decision process, investment decisions can involve the collation of data from a number of sources within a complex organisation. Typically these decisions move to and fro amongst many decision subsystems. We find, therefore, that the occurrence of the 'final act' of decision-making by a group of individuals is difficult to pinpoint. Also the passage of the decision through different parts of the organisation may be fragmented and unpredictable. King goes on to use the analogy of a 'legal court' – where there is a case for the prosecution and a case for the defence within an adversarial system. One manager describes this as: 'We are here to manage and to take the judgement of a reasonable man. If you look around at what other reasonable men do, we see that this is the sort of basis on which they normally make their judgements.' Barwise *et al* (1988)[6] suggest, however, that the decision process is somewhat disorderly. Their account of the decision-making process gives one the firm impression of a 'game' being played. In the 'game', the stakes for individual managers are their future careers just as much as the strategic or financial measures of subsequent business performance.

Barwise *et al*'s later account provides us with a rich metaphor (which we have called a 'game') used to uncover the perceived 'rules' at work. These revealed 'rules' may indicate that what we believe is important (for example, beating a financial hurdle) is not so important in some situations. (For instance, often *who* is involved in putting forward a project might be more important than the analytical justification for the decision).

Turning next to the theme of learning, past thinking on investment appraisal pays relatively little attention to investment appraisal as a *learning* process. This is even though managers are involved – inevitably – in intensive learning throughout the decision-making process. There are only a few significant exceptions to silence in past thinking on this subject. King, for instance, emphasises the importance of continual redefinition of the project through the appraisal process (but again this is a prescriptive suggestion, rather than descriptive observation). Barwise *et al* suggest that the appraisal process involves a learning process for decision-makers. And as already seen, Ghemawat highlights the importance of a 'learning rate' in the decision-making and implementation process. He compares this rate with the rate of build up of commitment in investment in a strategy – in many cases this might be much faster than the rate of learning.

SUMMARY

To summarise the implications of major investment decisions, we can draw the following conclusions:

- Major investment decisions typically involve ill-structured, rather than well-structured, problem-solving processes.
- They involve solving difficult analytical problems of a 'content' nature. This task needs to be accomplished within an organisational environment which is itself in flux.

- Decisions are channelled in varying and often unpredictable ways through these organisations.
- They also involve highly complex individual and organisational learning (which is akin to Argyris' 'double-loop learning' (1977),[7] where managers are trying to do new tasks, sometimes involving new skills, rather than learning to do old tasks more efficiently).

The final part of this chapter now contains a short case study drawn from a major technology group. The objective of this is to emphasise the more theoretical points made already in this chapter from a very practical point of view.

Short case study – Biotech International

Biotech International (BIT) was a newly founded division of a conglomerate technology-related group with a current turnover classifying it as a 'medium-sized business'. BIT was set up in order to exploit an existing market which was assumed to be just about to be transformed by a new technology.

Conglomerate plc (or 'CNG') supported the ambitious growth strategy embarked on by BIT. Although CNG was already advanced in developing its new technology, BIT lacked a market and operating base to exploit this in an international business sense.

BIT's growth was mapped out in a 'strategy for development' which sought an international position through acquisition. This strategy was implemented by a series of acquisitions based on a combination of deliberate targeting and capture of specific opportunities which came its way. During this expansion programme, the commitment to the strategy in the tangible form of financial investment built up considerably faster than the speed at which the management team could learn about the underlying competitive position of its businesses and equally the attractiveness of the industry which it was expanding into. This resulted in some significant problems in integration which began to undermine credibility of the strategy, especially in the eyes of CNG group management. This triggered an internal review by BIT divisional management, and a number of issues emerged from their review of the appraisal process of BIT's strategic investment programme. These are described as follows.

Acquisitions

It became clear that the pursuit of target acquisitions had become too frenetic an activity. During the rush to meet strategic objectives for growth the financial appraisal appeared merely to follow-on from, and to justify, decisions which had already been partially committed on 'strategic grounds'. Yet it was apparent that the view contained within the earlier 'strategy' was, in effect, becoming increasingly dated. This 'strategic vision' was also not detailed enough nor focused sufficiently on the particular product/markets which specific acquisition targets related to. Managers realised that they had been concentrating principally on the justification of NPVs, primarily based on internal assumptions, with the strategic evaluation being confined to vaguer notions of 'strategic fit'. These analytical problems were further complicated by the pressure to justify longer-term financial decisions very quickly indeed in the decision process.

R & D

BIT was also investing considerable sums in R&D and sought to incorporate the DCF techniques which were used in its parent CNG. Managers then formulated assumptions on market size. However, BIT's assumed market share and margins were notional and illustrative and were not supported by explicit assumptions on underlying competitive conditions and achievable competitive position. It was then decided to spend far more time and effort on exploring the *competitive* context of strategic investment decisions to lend more credence to 'the financial numbers'.

The value of the business unit strategies

Besides acquisitions, the second most important focus was on formulating a three-year financial plan. CNG group's philosophy was that a 'strategic plan' was *not* required every year. A strategic review was only required either when *a)* the business environment had been seen as having radically shifted, or *b)* where longer-term financial performance had fallen from milestones agreed with CNG. This meant that the primary vehicle for resource allocation (unless defined as 'capital' or as 'acquisitions') was made through the medium-term operating plan. But this operating plan was also framed in *accounting* rather than *economic* measures. The accounting basis for the plan meant that the economic value of the component business strategies was not therefore used as the focus for management decision-making. As a result, managers' efforts were primarily concentrated on producing a smoother medium-term operating and financial profile. Changes within the resource allocation process were then made incrementally, rather than being built up from a zero-base. This process was found particularly difficult to change even though BIT division was a youthful organisation: resource allocation systems and styles of appraisal had become quickly embedded.

Several lessons can be drawn from the above case:

1. The main problems in the decision-making process appear to be:

    –   the difficulty of exposing rather than burying major uncertainty;
    –   the problem of 'too much of the wrong kind of information and not enough of the right kind' (especially external and competitive);
    –   rapidly escalating commitment. Finally, time pressures can become chronic in dealing with a stream of acquisitions and may result in managers concentrating principally on rushing through longer-term financial decisions rather than on deeper probing of competitive and financial fundamentals.

2. Managers may seek to absorb uncertainty by appealing to prior strategic reviews (regardless of how up-to-date or thorough, or how relevant these are to the specific decision). Other 'uncertainty sponges' frequently brought into use by managers are the apparently 'scientific methods' of financial appraisal and financial modelling.

3. Medium-term plans and budgets are typically accounting-based and thus can further distort the resource allocation process. Also, the number and range of decision systems in place (strategic reviews, capital cases, acquisition cases, R&D appraisals, and medium-term plans) can give the illusion that 'everything is being covered'. But in practice this may result in fragmentation of insight, rather than cohesion of vision.

4. Without a coherent framework which integrates strategic and financial appraisal linked to subsequent controls, there is little to prevent sponsorship of particular strategies being more influenced by personal goals than by more objective, business analysis.

CONCLUSION

In this short chapter we have again highlighted the fact that the environment for decision-making is hostile to elaborate analytical techniques, save for the need for uncertainty – absorbing tools or 'sponges'. These can be derived from strategic or financial tools or from both – but this does not mean that analytical tools and processes should be jettisoned. Rather, it highlights the need to provide managers with the smallest number of tools which is consistent with producing a coherent vision and value for a particular opportunity. This needs to be accomplished also within the typically short time scales which are available at critical phases of the management process when a decision needs to be made.

This now takes us to a stage where we can see how these linkages between strategic and financial appraisal can be explored in practice as we begin to look at the research cases of Rolls Royce, IDV, London Underground and Post Office Counters and the additional case on BP in Chapters 6 to 8.

REFERENCES

1. Quinn, J B (1980) *Strategies for Change – Logical Incrementalism*, Richard D Irwin, Illinois

2. Ghemawat, P (1991) *Commitment, the Dynamic of Strategy*, The Free Press, Macmillan, New York

3. Mintzberg, H (1987) 'Patterns in Strategy Formation', *Management Science*, pp 934–48, May

4. Horovitz, J (1984) 'New Perspectives on Strategic Management', *Journal of Business Strategy*, vol 4, no 3, pp 19–33, Winter

5. King, P (1975) 'Is the Emphasis of Capital Budgeting Theory Misplaced?', *Journal of Business Finance and Accounting*, vol 2, no 1, pp 69–82

6. Barwise, P, Marsh, P, Thomas, K and Wensley, R (1988) *Managing Strategic Investment Decisions in Large Diversified Companies*, London Business School Paper

7. Argyris, C (1977) 'Double loop learning in organisations', *Harvard Business Review*, pp 115–25, September–October

PART 2 – PROBLEMS AND PERSPECTIVES

6

CASE ON INVESTMENT DECISIONS – ROLLS ROYCE AND GRAND MET (IDV)

INTRODUCTION

This case contains managers' perspectives on investment decisions from both Rolls Royce and IDV. As a joint case, it highlights the similarities and differences of two major private sector businesses. The case is set out as follows:

- Background to the case
- Value of investment decisions
- Uncertainty and interdependency
- Decision processes
- Controls
- Subjective judgement
- Practical lessons from the case
- Conclusions.

BACKGROUND TO THE CASE

Rolls Royce Aeroengines (RR) invests substantial sums in product research, development and launch, in acquisitions and joint ventures; in building positions in a particular country, in capturing key customers; in capital spending and in systems infrastructure. Rolls Royce managers focus mainly on problems associated with product development and launch, technology development and in market development – these areas being ones with high uncertainty and interdependency. The two managers involved from Rolls Royce were Simon Hart, corporate planning manager, and Austin Brackin, business planning manager, Military Engines Division.

International Distillers and Vintners (IDV) is one of the world's largest (alcoholic) drinks companies. IDV spends large sums annually on global brand development and support – a large fraction of which is of a long-term and essentially 'investment' nature. In addition to brand development, IDV is a frequent acquirer of businesses and makes ongoing investment in processing and distribution capacity together with office and IT infrastructure. The two managers involved in this case are David Shephard (IDV Europe) and Doug Waddell (IDV UK). In the months immediately prior to this research David Shephard was Finance Director of IDV (UK). David Shephard thus describes past experiences both at IDV (UK) and current issues at IDV (Europe).

In this composite chapter, issues are shared between Rolls Royce and IDV. Some issues, such as country position, contingent or opportunity value, terminal value, role of the directors, subjective judgement, are exclusive to Rolls Royce managers' perspectives. Others, such as brands, internal interdependency and marginal analysis are surfaced purely by IDV. When reading this case it may be useful for the reader to reflect on the question: '*To what extent are Rolls Royce's and IDV's problems of appraisal caused by a lack of explicit linkages of strategic and financial appraisal?*'

VALUE OF INVESTMENT DECISIONS

This section focuses on financial measurement of the 'worth' of investment decisions. Subsequent sections deal with the additional problems posed by uncertainty and interdependency.

The key areas explored by managers on value include the impact of investment decisions; brands and acquisitions; valuing country position; the base case; protective investment and value; intangibles; contingent and opportunity value; shareholder value and terminal value. This section contains, therefore, not only the problems of financial evaluation of a range of different kinds of investment decision, but also examines how value may arise for a particular decision in different ways.

Impact of investment decisions

The 'impact of investment decisions' covers not only 'what types of investment decisions are being made, but also *how* they relate to the business structure. Simon Hart (RR) reflects group discussions that 'investment' decisions span a much wider range than purely 'capital' ones:

> It seems to me that we are probably going to have to educate those in our companies that when money goes out of the door it is a cash item, irrespective of whether it is capital or revenue . . . What you are investing in is your future.

Simon then considers some dilemmas about the inherent differences in profitability between Rolls Royce's business structure – civil and military businesses:

> We have civil and military businesses. You might separate out the civil business and stick it in a corner. You might then discount the military projects at, well, let's just say some very low rate – say 3 or 4 per cent because it was such a low risk . . . whereas in the civil business you'd actually discount at some huge rate, to reflect a higher risk. Surely the obligation is to chase the one with the highest likely return?

The issue of how decisions fit into the business structure is also important for IDV. Doug Waddell (IDV) goes on to surface some broad links between competitive strategy and (implicitly) the impact on financial performance:

> What advantages are there from having a more focused portfolio? It is an interesting question. Well we would have tackled it before but I don't think that we ever have or ever would come out with the answer that we are entirely satisfied.

This hints at the possibility of increasing *distraction* costs arising where there is an incremental and ongoing investment in product development which increases business complexity. These may reach a point where there are significant intangible costs of distraction.

Brands and acquisitions

The issue of brands arises only for IDV managers, therefore this section deals exclusively with IDV.

An important area of evaluation is investment in *brands*. These are not capitalised but are clear examples of long-term investment involving significant lags between cash outflows and inflows. Doug Waddell (IDV) surfaces evaluation issues: 'Approximately £Xm per annum is spent on brands in Europe but this cannot easily be split between long- and short-term.'

IDV also invests in acquiring brands: Doug Waddell (IDV) says: 'People are paying very high prices [now] for brands because it takes so long to develop them . . . Brands like Martell have a tremendous following.'

Problems arise in planning and evaluating the efforts of brand spend for IDV:

> One debate is whether we should automatically spend Xp per case sold on supporting advertising spend. But it is very difficult; you can't be sure you could come up with a situation where this doesn't have much effect.
>
> (Doug Waddell)

> On the other hand you may have other measures . . . of increasing market share . . . we do test commercially, so there is that level of analysis, but it isn't all brought together.
>
> (David Shephard)

In order to make sense of the value of investment to develop brands into the future, Doug Waddell (IDV) draws on lessons from past experiences, especially on the notable success of Bailey's liqueur:

> The creme liqueur, it created a category of what else could it compete with.
>   I think that the great advantage that we had with Bailey's was that no one else was doing it.

Turning now to *acquisitions*, which embrace investment in both tangible and less tangible value, David Shephard reflects on how IRRs are set:

> How do we actually get to IRRs for acquisitions? In my experience it varies from anything between 15 per cent and 20 per cent . . . Acquisition B and B . . . yes, that project was taking out costs . . . about taking distribution costs and so it was seen as lower risk.

This suggests that the IRR hurdle varies for IDV acquisitions depending on perceived risk (see later section on risk). Doug Waddell (IDV) also says: 'I think that project appraisal process isn't too bad. Apart from [evaluating] the value lost if we don't acquire.' The issue of 'value lost' also appears linked to managers' (later) ideas of the *protective value* of an investment and evaluation of the base case (see forthcoming sections).

Valuing country position

Austin Brackin identifies the valuation of *country position* as a key issue and Simon Hart reflects on the uncertainty which surrounds this appraisal at Rolls Royce:

> One of the things which we find quite difficult to measure, because we have never done it (it is very subjective), is to say, 'What is it worth to build

positions in countries in Europe?' There aren't any ready-made markets where you can say 'I will go there tomorrow, I will build a huge plant and design it.' It just isn't like that.

(Austin Brackin)

It has always been subjective, evaluating the worth of doing business in that [wherever] country, recognising that it will be an important plant in the future even if you can't put a [current] value on it.

(Simon Hart)

Country investment is thus yet another slice of the 'investment cake' which managers find hard to evaluate, partly because it cuts across other analyses of investment and revenue and cost analysis, and also because of the length of time that investment might be for and the uncertainty surrounding the benefits and interdependencies.

Turning back to IDV, although the possibility of identifying *opportunity value* also surfaces, this appears peripheral in managers' thinking about valuation:

We don't look at valuing a new brand in terms of the total potential set of opportunities, as really the marketability of that brand at that stage is so uncertain.

The base case

Austin Brackin of Rolls Royce flags up the problem of assessing the shape of the base case:

Simon, in our business, inevitably the market will be going down. It is inevitable, isn't it? So many, many manufacturing industries at the forefront of technology are in a situation where, inevitably, if you do nothing, someone will overtake you.

It's inevitable that unless we do R&D then we will gradually go into decline. But by how much? It may be over a very long time. But it *is* inevitable.

This is echoed by Simon Hart:

Actually, I think that most of our assumptions are that if we do nothing, then nothing will happen.

If we went into the market with a radically improved engine – with vastly improved fuel consumption . . . then the guy who bought our competitor's (inferior) engine would fail in the market place just through the difference between performance.

The argument comes down to, if you don't do this, you won't be in the game in so many years' time. And the accountant would . . . he doesn't know how to evaluate it.

Rolls Royce's views are in contrast with those of IDV. Doug Waddell reflects on a past experience where some managers claimed that the base case was in decline. He describes how this received a somewhat frosty reception:

> We'd say, OK, if we develop the pub to this point then returns will take off, rather than taking the difference between that increase and a static view of current revenues we assume a decline. Now that got them into much trouble, terrible trouble because it was very easy for us to say that therefore anything you can do will make money, so the incremental analysis was very dangerous from a pure financial point of view.

These contrasting views may be due to a variety of factors including differences in the rate and shape of competitive and technology change between these two industries, and variations in appraisal and control style. Nevertheless, regardless of the approach taken to the base case, the question remains as to how the rate of decline can be predicted and measured. This raises questions about what strategic or operational alternatives are available besides the financial value of this range of options, to which we will later return.

Protective investment and value

The comments on *protective investment* came from Rolls Royce. Simon Hart reflects that 'By investing in one project, you may be guaranteeing the success of project B *and* project C.' Austin Brackin (RR) relates 'protective investment' to the strategy of seeking a wide customer base:

> Now only one of those (customers) collapsing, as we saw in fact in 1971, can cause the whole structure to crumble. The only thing that you can do is to protect yourself by having a much wider customer base . . .

Austin Brackin also highlights the value and volatility of customer base:

> In some businesses – I think I was saying this to someone last night – in some businesses like IDV you have a very wide customer base and no single, individual thing can destroy that . . . it is terribly difficult to destroy the whole base at one go.

The above emphasises that where value in a business is dependent on highly uncertain variables, then *incremental* value can be captured often most effectively by protective investment rather than necessarily by investment which extends the scope (and thereby vulnerability) of the business.

Intangibles

Simon Hart of Rolls Royce considers that intangibles are things which may, at some stage, have a measurable value:

> Isn't the principle of these intangible benefits that, one day, in the far distant future, they will actually materialise?
>
> It's a strange system where you don't try to quantify the benefits, otherwise you are hard-pressed to justify why you are doing it.

But he then goes on to describe some potential difficulties in evaluating intangibles in financial terms:

> I am not sure that we would want to rush into it [measuring intangibles] . . . Getting the message across, understood so that the decision can be made, is a complex process. If you make the decision so full of intangibles, then it becomes almost impossible [laughs] to make the decision, because you make such a fog of it. There is quite a fine line between plastering it with uncertainty and quantifying numbers.

Austin Brackin then focuses on the need for honesty and integrity in dealing with intangibles:

> It depends on the integrity with which you can genuinely say the intangibles have been assessed. It's David's [of IDV] argument again; if you don't actually genuinely believe that you've got a saving there then you can't, with integrity, include it.

Both IDV managers take a more cautious view of intangibles: Doug Waddell says, 'I am very nervous about a project which shows the majority of benefits which are soft.' David Shephard goes on to say:

> The space question . . . People put a machine into a space and unless there is some other decision, for example, you're going to knock the wall down or something, it's not going to be a real saving actually contributing to the profitability of the organisation. These are 'artificial' savings, such as the floor space which Rolls Royce has reduced from 103,000 square feet. But what happens if it is never used? Is that a difference in your [Rolls Royce] industry and ours? The thing that drives Grand Met is the bottom-line profit.

Simon Hart suggests that certain areas of so-called 'intangibles' can be managed through charging out for services within the business, especially those benefits associated with IT investment:

> We've got a charge-out mechanism . . . if you represent the full charge or

'funny money' accounting, it does actually help to reduce the overall investment that is required in computing.

This is echoed by David Shephard of IDV who reflects on approaches to measuring changes in less tangible areas – one application being, again, 'charging out' for use of resource and the other being 'counting out' for reducing levels of resource and thus cost:

> I was very anti-charge out, but then we said, that computer is such a vast quantity . . . that really did force them . . . They started looking at (costs), which led to real decisions on revising systems.
>
> That project, we generate these savings, and if we do, yes, that was the judgement, that we would be able to count the people out of that department, that section.

The above account of intangibles shows some sharply contrasting approaches by IDV and Rolls Royce. This appears to reflect divergences of control and measurement systems and appraisal styles which are deeply embedded in organisational behaviour and attitudes.

Contingent and opportunity value

First, at Rolls Royce Simon Hart explores the value inherent in technology as having *contingent* value:

> A problem was solved by borrowing technology from another part of the Group. In a way, that could have been put on the shelf and not used but we were able to come back, find it and use it.
>
> How do you value technology, when you are being asked to come in and participate in a joint venture . . . we have had a lot of fun and games trying to decide what we are worth . . . ? When you are actually lending your name to something and it is your technology, er, we've had quite a lot of thinking to do to decide what it is that we bring to the party.

Austin Brackin also adds the example of a joint venture as *opportunity* value:

> We said, effectively to the Board direct, and in addition you must bear in mind you may have opportunities in this, you may have opportunities in that, so there are pluses. And that you could add another X to the whole scenario. But you can't actually say there's a 30 per cent chance that you will get that opportunity.
>
> We have an opportunity to be involved in the setting up of a new industry in country X. Taking that opportunity actually changes the whole pattern of rivalry in that country . . . It may have uncovered opportunities that

formerly we weren't well placed to take as a spin-off from that particular project.

For Rolls Royce, contingent and opportunity value thus emerge as being very important sources of value which require explicit management. This is made more tricky because this value is considered to be too uncertain and hard to define to incorporate within financial planning and control systems.

Shareholder value

Simon Hart (RR) explores the idea of shareholder value:

> I like the concept of valuing a bit of business, not just a project. I mean a whole operating unit, and be able to say, what's the kind of strategy we are into, what is it worth?'
>
> So what I did was plot what the project does, the NPV of the first five years against the NPV over the next five years . . . Obviously the older projects have got a pretty high NPV. I found it quite helpful, seeing whether the share price stacked up against the value of the projects. It was really a way to communicate to our own management the value of projects . . . It was quite a convenient shorthand way of marrying, certainly our corporate plan, with the underlying value of the strategy. The value of the strategy is this, plus that, plus that, plus all of those over the life. If it doesn't match up [with the share price] then we've got a problem; someone else can come in and pay more for it.

This experimentation with valuing business strategies and project groupings appears to have led on to a subsequent shift in Rolls Royce's decision processes. Since 1989 Simon Hart and the planning team have gone on to apply some of these techniques to a number of major investment decisions.

Simon Hart (RR) also links the use of shareholder value and valuation of business strategy techniques to corporate finance theory:

> You talk about the capital asset pricing model, the value of your company doubles or halves depending upon how you perceive the discount rate to apply . . . I think discount rates are such a huge factor, particularly when you are compared with a lot of Europe . . . there is a tendency to apply UK-based rates to those calculations as opposed to trying to apply a European one, and it has a huge impact on perceptions of the business value.

The above extracts reveal that cost of capital (particularly relative cost of capital) *can* become important in certain situations. These may occur when competitors have a perceived lower cost of capital *and* when the industry requires long time horizons for investment. These circumstances give competitors a *financial* competitive advantage.

Terminal value

Again, terminal value is raised as an issue mainly by Rolls Royce managers who deal with investments with (typically) longer time horizons than IDV. Simon Hart explains:

> You are actually looking at a project and taking it out to the end of its life; well, fine. That's a rather luxurious position to have, total knowledge. But if you say, we'll take it out ten years and you have to do something with that tenth year, then as sure as night follows day it has got to have *some* value. I worry about residual value just being the sustainable cash flow at your five [years], which you then assume goes on for ever.
>
> You take the cash flow (let's assume that it continues beyond five years) and, er, you divide it by the discount rate. It sort of devalues the whole process. You go into great detail for each year and then . . . [cuts off].

Here Simon Hart highlights a problem of 'NPV infection': where a good part of the NPV resides in a terminal value and where managers have not probed the basis for this value in-depth, then this, covertly or overtly may undermine the ultimate valuation.

Commentary on both groups of managers' perspectives on value:

- For both Rolls Royce and IDV, investment decisions are seen not merely as 'capital' but also as including acquisitions and long-term investment such as in R&D and brands.
- The relative complexity and diversity of business structure is a factor in both companies making appraisal more difficult.
- Brands pose a particularly difficult problem for IDV: although in many ways they are comparable with Rolls Royce's R&D problems, brands are inherently less tangible. IDV's planning and control systems also appear more focused on the short-term than Rolls Royce's and managers are finding more tactical methods of appraisal unsuited to resource allocation of brand development spend. There are pointers to seeking more externally orientated and broader-based measures but the application of these ideas appears to require significant change of existing planning and control processes and appraisal style.

Steps were taken by IDV subsequent to the research to explore changes in this area.

- Acquisitions posed a major issue for IDV and involved a mix of tangible and less tangible elements. IDV managers appeared a lot more comfortable in dealing with appraisal of acquisitions than for brands, perhaps partly because they could use financial modelling techniques here more extensively.

- The value of a country position was an explicit issue for Rolls Royce, as country-specific investment for RR was perhaps more intensive than for IDV in the form of plant, joint ventures etc. This area generated difficulty because it related to a bundle of tangible and less tangible areas of investment and also because the time horizons for investment were very long. Finally it involved a number of major competitive uncertainties and interdependencies.

- The base case posed a major problem for both companies. Rolls Royce appeared more receptive to, and more relaxed with, the idea of underpinning a declining base case in financial terms by appropriate competitive assumptions. IDV, in contrast, were far more hesitant and cautious as this, they feared, might open the path to justifying all kinds of investment on the basis of 'if we don't do it, this is the negative effect'. IDV managers pointed out, however, that this factor is indeed taken into account when evaluating acquisitions which would secure and build on an existing business base.

- Protective value appears crucial for Rolls Royce managers as the business itself is 'fragile' in that it depends on maintaining a number of major customers in key segments.

- Intangibles were recognised by both Rolls Royce and IDV, but managers from both companies (especially IDV) were uncomfortable with the idea of intangibles as 'non-measured value'. Performance measurement and reward systems appear to be an important influence on managers' willingness to put a value on imprecise benefits.

- Contingent and opportunity value were also very important issues at Rolls Royce. This was because of external reshaping of markets and a shift towards increasing collaborative arrangements, and the potential for extending the use of existing technology internally. Although 'opportunity value' exists for IDV too, for example in exploiting existing brands under development through new markets and channels, it was not felt by IDV managers to be appropriate to incorporate a value for these zones of value formally because these options were felt to be 'too unpredictable'.

- Shareholder value was an issue which came up for the Rolls Royce corporate planner, who experimented during the research with valuing business strategies and major substrategies. This method of linking financial and strategic appraisal appeared to be fruitful for Simon Hart.
- Finally, terminal value emerged as a kind of 'black box' at the end of the time horizon of detailed forecasts. This was a particular concern for Rolls Royce. It raised questions of how strategic appraisal can be used to steer judgements on how that terminal value can be arrived at meaningfully.

UNCERTAINTY AND INTERDEPENDENCY

This section looks at external uncertainty, competitor intent, risk assessment, external and internal interdependencies, the alignment of variables driving value and finally, knock-on effects.

External uncertainty

Simon Hart describes the assumed problems of linking prospects for an individual project and Rolls Royce's view of industry trends as a whole:

> When you make an individual launch, you don't usually try to predict the direction of the whole industry, you look at that later. If you are selling an engine of a particular size to a sector you make some assumptions about the growth of the sector; you have to make some assumptions about other sales which may have an impact on that sector.

Simon Hart reflects on the potential impact of international change:

> We all know in the military business that peace might break out . . . For each set of conditions, there's a whole series of assumptions you can make about your position in there.

The volatility of international conditions affecting demand is highlighted in stark relief by Austin Brackin. The first research sessions coincided with political upheaval in Eastern Europe in late 1989. Austin Brackin considers his own and Simon Hart's reaction to this, only several weeks later:

> When we sat down at Cranfield two or three weeks ago, we could not have anticipated what has happened in East Germany, to take an example, which could have a major impact on our business by 1993–94.

But besides these macro- and industry level uncertainties, we also see another layer of uncertainty impacting on each individual product launch:

I think the problem is, we have two big imponderables. The market is one, the actual cost of developing the engine is the other, with the timescales and inherent technological risk. By the time you've put these two together, you've got a nonsense – effectively – if you try to do a statistical analysis of that.

(Austin Brackin)

We have got a billion dollar business here, which effectively invests in an intrinsically risky area, where, say, your share of specific sectors in the market could range between 20 and 80 per cent.

(Simon Hart)

Although IDV faces apparently a much lower degree of external uncertainty, there are factors, nevertheless, which cloud business (and thus individual brand) prospects. Doug Waddell says: 'We have a huge problem with substitutes because of the problem with the health lobby, soft drinks.' During the research both IDV managers came to realise that 'The thing we don't spend a lot of time on is the external environment'(David Shephard). 'I don't think we spend that much time on the external assumptions at all, except where they directly affect us' (Doug Waddell). This realisation was subsequently a factor in triggering efforts to upgrade the outward-looking focus of planning systems in a number of areas in IDV.

But both groups of managers appear to lack tools through which they can gain greater clarity on these uncertainties. In particular at Rolls Royce, Simon Hart says:

We have used scenarios . . . we have had 'highs' and 'lows'. Our tendency was to shoot for the one in the middle. It somewhat devalued the process and we don't do that any longer . . . we didn't feel that we wanted to put more and more numbers or lines on pictures that made it look even more complex and confusing.'

Almost with prescience (now looking back from the early 1990s to late 1989) Simon Hart shows a keenness in finding tools or measures through which managers can extend their time horizons when he says, 'There ought to be indicators for most of our business that would tell there was going to be an [economic] downturn.'

External uncertainty is thus clearly a very important factor impacting on value. Yet where there are major discontinuities in the industry environment, managers find it hard to adjust their world view quickly so that the implications for strategy and the value of the strategy can be appreciated.

This highlights the stickiness of perceptions of both the strategy and its financial value.

Competitor intent

As a specific area of uncertainty, *competitor intent* emerges as an important variable. Simon Hart (RR), reflecting on a past experience of an unsuccessful product launch, raises the matter of competitor intent:

> It was an attractive market . . . I don't think that any of us dreamt that the competitor's response would be a completely new engine . . . that really messed up the economics of that whole business case.

He also hints that competitor myopia may be common rather than the exception:

> Sometimes our suppliers say, we've talked to all three of you, and your requirements add up to 150 per cent of the market . . . You've probably got everybody trying to get a better share than they have got now.

But Simon Hart (RR) in reflecting on the importance of competitor intent is cautious that 'Competitor analysis is a bit of a minefield anyway . . . it is an industry in its own right, you can have vast amounts of data.'

Doug Waddell of IDV also gives some further insights into why competitor analysis is often relatively ineffective:

> We recognise that we are relatively weak at competitor analysis. A lot of it is word of mouth but not documented. We are going on third or fourth party statements which may or may not be true. So we have to concoct a readily organised procedure for administering it.

But one case where managers have used competitor analysis with good effect emerges, Austin Brackin of Rolls Royce recalls:

> We did actually do some written assessments of the effects [for a particular strategic decision] on competitors and customers. We did actually put some things down and try to assess what the effect was likely to be.

Managers thus appear to be ambivalent to competitor analysis, seeing it as 'the logical thing to do' on the one hand, but inhibited from experimentation by the need to invest further effort in the process without having assured benefits.

Risk assessment

Simon Hart (RR) reflects on *risk* that:

What we don't do, and this is probably because, perhaps, we are not confident in our own abilities and those of the people reviewing the outputs in our process, is assigning statistical probabilities. Perhaps our operational researchers would know what to do, but in the commercial world we wouldn't know how to handle that . . . maybe it's just not within our culture.

Simon Hart indicates that Rolls Royce perceive different levels of risk depending on the nature of the project:

The risk associated with a military product, provided that you get an appropriate launch customer which is Government, is fairly low. On the civil side, it is a different matter.

Austin Brackin also tells us how he approaches the evaluation of more than one key variable through plotting two variables against one another to see the effect on the IRR (see Figure 6.1). This tool highlights the relative sensitivity of NPV to two different key variables in the slope of the curve. It also indicates how much leeway projections have over and above break-even (NPV projections):

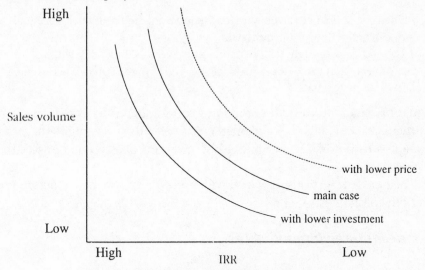

Figure 6.1 The carpet plot – illustration

What the carpet plot says is that if we have estimated the development spend, then what is the effect of this. If we have got this wrong on the carpet plot then you can look at the effect of this at the same time as if you have got a bigger market. So it is relatively simple to look at the effect.

(Austin Brackin)

IDV also face considerable difficulties in deciding how to evaluate risk. For instance, David Shephard (IDV) reflects again on a particular UK acquisition. He appears puzzled about why internal savings are generally perceived to be 'lower risk':

> Most of the savings came out of integration which was seen as low risk.
>
> For example, if you say 'you can take thirty people out', you can actually say 'where are they?' So the risk associated is actually lower. Maybe this is wrong. It does sound as if this is odd.

Austin Brackin (RR) describes the appraisal linked to risk:

> You've got to put some conservatism in somewhere, some reserve, something or other. You do that either by upping the hurdle rate or the discount rate . . . .

This is contrasted by Doug Waddell (IDV):

> So you are, I guess, talking about the risk of the project itself, not about the risk of the financing costs or the risk inherent in the makeup of the business.
>
> The cost of finance covers you for the inherent nature of your business, it doesn't cover you for project risk.
>
> I would have thought that there are other ways with dealing with risk of the project. You can flex your model and get a range. You can take some sort of range for that.

What managers from both companies reveal, therefore, is that risk is a particularly difficult area for managers to deal with. It also highlights how easy it is to be drawn into hiking the discount rate to compensate for project risk.

The next few sections now deal with perspectives on interdependency in both companies:

External interdependencies

Simon Hart of Rolls Royce suggests that market demand and airline fleet strategy are closely interdependent:

> To sell the concept of the regional airliner you need to understand how it can be integrated into fleets, whereas in the big markets you rely on Boeing to tell you . . .

He then reflects on the apparent stickiness of demand – once an airline begins buying it can lead on to sales of other engines:

> Airline X decided to buy the Y engine. That was the first time they had

bought Rolls Royce for 20 years. It wasn't long before they came in and bought other smaller aircraft engines. I don't think it is by any means certain that they would have done the second purchase had they not done the first.

He goes on to describe how product linkages can affect value through the value of a whole being greater than the value of parts:

If we make a policy decision that we aren't going to cover all the market, then part of the evaluation has to say, well, if we don't cover all the market then we will lose some of the customer base that we have already got.

It may be quite wrong to justify each product in isolation because it may be that the most important thing of all is to develop a range of products because it is the range that you are selling.

But it has not proved easy to model these product linkages to assess potential financial impact, says Simon, 'We haven't played some master business game, what happens if one wins and that one doesn't, what happens to the various sectors?' This may also be relevant to interdependencies between present and future market conditions. He reflects:

If you were going to invest some money in product X . . . and the mere fact that you are positioning that may add to your cash stream, but it could easily be an excellent launch pad for something in the future, without that launch pad you couldn't have that at all.

Although IDV managers do not have quite as many examples as Rolls Royce of external interdependency, David Shephard draws one close parallel:

Malibu arrived when pina colada was fashionable, and it just complemented it. That helped enormously. But otherwise I don't know why it has been so successful.'

External interdependencies are thus perceived to be very important at Rolls Royce but there appear to be major problems in mapping what these interdependencies are likely to be, how they impact on specific decisions and also how these may be actively managed. These management issues are aggravated again because financial planning and control systems do not readily lend themselves to assessment of 'softer' areas of value.

Internal interdependencies

Whilst Rolls Royce managers majored on external interdependencies, it is now IDV's turn to highlight *internal* interdependencies, especially those within financial models and budgets. David Shephard starts by saying

'The model, the lot of paper, I think it was *that* thick. The assumptions were all interdependent.'

Another issue closely related to internal interdependency is the relationship between individual parts of the investment project, especially where the financial appraiser's job is to justify not merely the project as a whole but actively to seek out alternatives. He describes the situation in country D, where local managers are seeking to expand existing capacity:

> I have difficulty in persuading them, for example, that we can use the equipment more efficiently.
>
> And then you start actually looking at the viability of the operation; it leads you to looking at this potential for divestment as opposed to staying in.

He also comments later that:

> The one in country D is again interesting. We said, let's look at it again. The investment requirement has halved. You are then doing just what is necessary, you are not investing in future capacity. Yet you have to leave your options open, so you can justify future capacity.

David Shephard then reflects on this same project (in country D) and applies the idea of disaggregating a project to its constituent elements:

> If you start to break the project down, there is a bit to do with the expansion of facilities. But we already have enough capacity, and expansion might produce greater shock. So there is a real dilemma, there is a real difficulty in quantifying what the benefits are . . .

Ultimately David Shephard's sustained probing of this proposal using financial tools and by raising both operational and strategic questions led to its reformulation as a much more financially attractive project. This also strengthened the existing country strategy without building in unnecessary fixed capacity.

Alignment and knock-on effects

Before we leave interdependency, another issue worth raising is that of *alignment* of factors driving value which links both external and internal variables. Simon Hart (RR) says:

> We'll actually say, if you want an engine of so many thousand pounds thrust then you have to have it developed. All you've done is some predevelopment work, but you won't have spent the real money. The real money comes when he says yes, I will have an aeroplane, I'm going to take

your engine, like that, and I've got a customer who I have lined up and who says he will buy 30 aircraft – and all these three factors line up.

Simon Hart also reflects on the impact of knock-on effects:

It is difficult to postulate what will happen if you don't do something. You can do the simple effects in financial terms, but you cannot always see the knock-on effects. We don't try to simulate the knock-on effect normally. But we did do some conscious appraisal when we were considering the ongoing development of the Y a few years ago.

Commentary on managers' perspectives on uncertainty and interdependency:

- Rolls Royce faces major external uncertainties in its industry structure, both in the civil and in the military business. In the military business managers faced considerable discontinuity following change in the Eastern Bloc. The speed at which this discontinuity became apparent put a major strain on managers' short-term ability to shift strategic assumptions.
- Although facing less cataclysmic change, IDV also faces imponderables, including the threat of substitutes which may impact on the value of business investment.
- For both companies competitor intent was an important issue. Rolls Royce managers, for example, could point to cases where competitors had made moves which had significantly destroyed the assumed value from an investment decision. A barrier towards competitor analysis was seen to be the amount of data required – it seems as if managers seek a comprehensive picture of competitor activity and intent which may not be available and not be (ultimately) cost effective. IDV also was keen on exploring competitor analysis and managers were anxious to move away from narrow, more tactically based assessments of competitors.
- Risk analysis was also important for managers from both companies. Rolls Royce managers felt that complex, risk analysis techniques had limited utility in practice, although they were using visual displays for highlighting the effect of two uncertain variables (the 'carpet plots'). At both Rolls Royce and IDV there were hints that hurdle rates were sometimes raised as one method of compensating for higher risk, although Doug Waddell (who was evidently well-schooled in financial theory) pointed out vigorously that sensitivity analysis was a more appropriate tool to make risk adjustments.

- Interdependencies were important for both Rolls Royce and IDV. At IDV the key areas were internal interdependency and the breaking down of a project into its constituent parts. At Rolls Royce some very important external interdependencies surfaced. These related to how demand crystallised over a period of years. The value of 'alignment' of a number of key factors driving value (both external and internal) for example in lining up a number of key drivers of customer demand, was also highlighted. This concept of 'alignment' may also be of application beyond the sale of aeroengines to many other industries with rapid technology and market change.

DECISION PROCESSES

This section focuses on the management processes involved in evaluating strategic investment decisions. It contains strategic objectives, decision criteria, valuing a business, the cost of capital, payback, financial and business modelling, marginal analysis, role of directors, prioritisation and financial constraints.

Strategic objectives

On *strategic objectives*, Doug Waddell (IDV) reflects on two related areas:

1. We then need to link the strategy to projects, and I think that that is relatively easy once the strategy is in place.
2. We've established a strategy which links to projects. We now need to measure progress towards an ultimate goal.

The above highlights that strategic objectives for major projects presupposes the existence of a strategy. Having strategic objectives then makes it feasible to set strategic controls. However, the benefit of setting strategic objectives for projects is that these help focus on how those projects *add value* to the strategy.

Decision criteria

Decision criteria vary between the kinds of decisions being considered and also between both organisations. First, Simon Hart of Rolls Royce:

> I can imagine some kinds of organisation are very numbers driven . . . you know, if the numbers didn't work then we don't go . . . whereas it is certainly not true in our organisation.

Simon Hart also reveals his discomfort with pure 'strategic' criteria:

> We can argue a thing on strategic grounds and actually in our hearts think that we will make money out of it. It seems rather that we are kidding ourselves if that is really what we mean by a strategic move. I am very cautious of this word 'strategy'. But I agree that that will have to improve or enhance our position even though, on the numbers today, we can't actually see our way through it.

David Shephard (IDV) then reveals that, whilst many investments are evaluated with tight financial measures, he perceives an apparent bias in organisational preferences. He observes that 'Perhaps we are more generous with brands because we are a brand-led organisation'.

This is mirrored in Rolls Royce's situation. Simon Hart explains that he thinks of it 'as capital expenditure; we have quite a different rate from project expenditure . . . we usually have different criteria.'

He then adds on *strategic criteria*:

> I don't know how we value this [speed to market] really. I don't think we knowingly put in a factor which says 'we are going to be first to get into this aeroplane so that we could get a third market share, or a sixth if we come in last.

Austin Brackin (RR) also indicates that *operational criteria* are important too, indicating that due to Rolls Royce's resource base being 'sticky' this has an inevitable influence on decision-making:

> If we employ a certain number of engineers, I don't know how many thousand, we know that we are going to spend a certain amount on the salaries of engineers over a period of time. That effectively creates a minimum figure that we are going to spend on R&D.

He then suggests that the communication of the strategy is a prerequisite for ensuring that operational criteria mesh with strategic criteria:

> Unless they, in operations, understand where the strategy is going, they can't necessarily flag up these things – expand, expand, expand, you know, the operational people may say hey, hang on, we can't do it.

Doug Waddell (IDV) also echoes this issue when he says 'The strategy must be communicated to the operational people and the operational people then are responsible for giving back-up.'

The above suggests that overall managers find it difficult to formulate clear and consistent criteria for decision-making which embrace strategic, financial and operational criteria.

Cost of capital

Managers from both organisations raise the cost of capital as an important issue. Simon Hart (RR) reflects on how to arrive at a cost of capital:

> Taking a weighted cost of capital might be right when you are looking at a twenty-year decision but it might be wrong when looking at three years' payback where you – I would think you would have to take a marginal cost of borrowing.

He then moves on to consider the utility of IRR, given the amount of uncertainty underpinning decisions. He also highlights the technical pitfalls of using IRR where cash flows are peculiar and are sometimes positive and sometimes negative in future years:

> We do a fair amount of work using IRR, but we recognise that it is fraught by potential forecasting error . . . We know it is very difficult to predict the market, so we use it in a sense as a secondary indicator as we can't use it as *the* 'hurdle'.
>
> I had an amusing situation . . . the finance person said to me, 'I don't like NPV s because I don't understand them, I prefer to look at IRRs, and so we went back to the computer to churn out the IRRs. And there were certain cash flows which were very strange . . . we got to the number 2,508 per cent [laughing]. We decided to stop.

Both IDV managers also describe possible difficulties in defining and applying the *cost of capital*:

> I think it [capital] is all considered to be marginal borrowings. Grand Met currently buys acquisitions for cash so we tend to use bank rate.

(David Shephard)

> But even that is inaccurate, because most of our borrowings are at 10 per cent.
>
> It is very difficult to calculate the cost in terms of share capital. What the share capital is actually costing you, or what the shareholder's expectation is, and that is dependent upon the type of business you are, and the type of risks you face.

(Doug Waddell)

Doug Waddell then describes how he helped derive the cost of capital during a consultancy project with Imperial Group prior to joining IDV:

> Personal experience has taught me that when you divide your businesses up and allocate to them differing costs of capital, as a result of perceived risks, is to over-intellectualise the situation. I think we could do without it

because at the end of the day if we are simply not willing to undertake certain projects, then businesses are going to fade away. It doesn't stand up logically.

This is where it [financial theory] all falls down; the subjective nature of the stockmarket, it survives a rumour and, er, perceived future.

David Shephard (IDV) identifies some difficulties in deciding which financial method to use (IRR or NPV), and when:

It is . . . the IRR and discounted cash flow. I get confused about what it is telling me. What happens if I do an IRR and I don't think I am sophisticated enough. I don't think I have enough knowledge of the techniques to say 'these are the differences' and this is how it will make the decision-taking process better.

Doug Waddell (IDV) tries to clarify this: 'If we are talking discounted cash flow, if we are making 10 per cent then we are making real money.' This highlights again that the appropriate use of financial tools (NPV and IRR) is not always self-evident to managers in practice, thus confirming past research.

The above debate on cost of capital and IRR highlights how central managers perceive the issue of financial hurdles to be. Although these issues are of importance there is a danger that managers become mesmerised by the technical issues. The ambiguity surrounding which tools to use may suggest that these problems are an important block on managers improving decision processes as so much energy and concern is tied up in this problem area.

Payback

In contrast, David Shephard (IDV) is less hesitant on the use of *payback*. He says, 'Payback, for all its weaknesses, is nice and simple [for capital investment].'

He then reflects on an experience of applying payback apparently as a targeting device:

So you are leaving your options open [in country D] . . . you are saying . . . I need to spend this amount of money to keep the previous operation. Maybe then you start to move towards a three-year payback.

Should you set totally different criteria for a replacement decision project to a cost reduction project, to putting in expanding capacity?

Doug Waddell (IDV) adds helpfully that, 'When you are investing in a company you probably need something a little more sophisticated. Not just DCF but also straight payback, I don't see any harm in highlighting other measures.' Turning to Rolls Royce, Austin Brackin states: 'I think we decided that having put a cap on capital expenditure, we couldn't afford more than X a year . . . we found we could get very short paybacks from some of the investments.'

Simon Hart (RR) then responds:

> If we can demonstrate that it [capital investment] has a payback of four years, then you know that it equates roughly to an acceptable rate of return without trying to be too clever about cash flows in years 6,7,8,9 and 10, which are fraught anyway . . . in that sense it is a capital rationing tool.

The above suggests that provided managers are aware of the consequences of using payback and apply it in the appropriate context, then it is not necessarily 'wrongful' to use it. The problem may occur, however, where simple and attractive measures like payback become habitual and drive out other measures. It may be difficult for managers to use a complete battery of tools – payback, IRR, NPV – all at the same time without a good deal of practice.

Financial and business modelling

Financial modelling surfaces as a tool which provides IDV financial managers with a framework for evaluating decisions. This gives them a key role in the decision-making process. David Shephard (IDV) says:

> Finance are the people who they could impact on the decision quite dramatically through their analysis. For acquisitions, the financial people build the models although the MD will say, yes, I agree with the assumptions.

But he also reflects on the apparent tendency towards over-sophistication resulting from the power of financial modelling tools:

> We do seem to prevaricate. We come back and make minor changes to the assumptions. At the end I guess we get down to things that matter in terms of the total context.

David Shephard points out the emphasis on accuracy and links this to the apparent stress in IDV on control and measurement:

> I think we try to be too clever, I don't know how you get the right balance because at the end you are expected to test your actuals against your assumptions.

The following describes how a complex acquisition case was modelled with great attention to the impact of (primarily) internal variables:

There is a lot of research work done on acquisitions . . . We went through and built a detailed model which identified incremental profitability in terms of additional volume and costs . . . We would look at the incremental sales force cost, production cost and central support costs. It would then have a similar model for cross-sales from retail so we get incremental profit . . .

(David Shephard)

Rolls Royce also use financial modelling extensively but, in addition, *external* variables appear as important concerns. Simon Hart explores the problems of trying to capture the impact of external variables in financial models:

We don't do an overall model of the industry to see what's happening out there when we try to justify a project targeted at a particular market. Maybe you can't do that; maybe it just produces another layer of subjectivity. I don't really know that we know how to process the risk calculations.

Simon Hart also indicated a keen interest in 'leading indicators' as precursors of external discontinuity. This again highlights the problem that Rolls Royce's investment programme demands commitment of funds beyond the time scale of 'ready foreseeability'.

But on a final note, Austin Brackin (RR) also points out that the panoply of strategic tools available to help explore the factors driving the value of an investment decision is such that:

The idea of going through the whole thing every time you wanted to make an investment decision would be horrifying . . . I think that from a practical point of view you are going to use these models as a sort of checklist.

Here managers appear to be meeting problems because they are trying to apply well- or semi-structured modelling tools to ill-structured problems. These problems are likely to be aggravated when predicting complex and interacting external variables where uncertainty compounds further into the future.

Role of the director

The issue of the 'role of the director' arose only for Rolls Royce, probably because both Rolls Royce managers involved in the study are below 'director level', whereas at IDV the managers are both financial directors. A particular issue which arose was the extent to which directors should be closely involved in the decision-making process. Both Rolls Royce managers recoil from the idea that Board level directors should be closely involved in more detailed assumptions:

> Directors are not there to sort out investment decisions, they are there to ensure that the calculations have been done, that someone has checked them all through and that they have been put together as a reasonable proposition that has been through the organisation.

(Austin Brackin)

> They [the directors] have to satisfy themselves that the relevant specialists have vetted it all the way through.

(Simon Hart)

> They are there to say should we be going into this at all.

(Austin Brackin)

In this instance, the 'Board of Directors' at Rolls Royce are distanced from initial compilation of fine detailed assumptions of major investment decisions. Senior management below Board level at Rolls Royce are extensively involved in putting together business cases, with Board directors probing key assumptions.

Prioritisation and financial constraints

Turning next to *prioritisation*, David Shephard explains that projects do not arrive in an orderly and steady sequence as implied by financial textbooks. This makes 'set piece' comparisons between projects hard to arrange:

> Tell me, I mean, within IDV, I guess you would have just one project at a time, and you don't actually get down to an A,B,C,D,E,F,G comparison of proposals. You've got one acquisition now, then probably in three months' time you have probably got another one.

The above suggests a picture of projects which are identified at fairly random intervals. This is also mirrored at Rolls Royce where it is said that 'strategic decisions do not occur every day of the week'. Unlike financial textbooks which are often written as if investment projects can be lined up for comparison like 'ducks in a row', more typically in practice managers have to judge individual projects on their own merits.

Moving next onto the issue of financial constraints, David Shephard (IDV) reflects that the 'earnings dilution' constraint implicitly means that there is pressure to avoid investment projects where returns are very long-term and remote:

Isn't there a real danger that you would have opportunity costs/benefits, you are putting in things for which you might have a return in ten years' time and the return on investment is going to be diluted?

This suggests an uneasy coexistence of the *economic* bases for longer-term decision making, against the underlying *accounting* bases of reporting short- and medium-term earnings.

Concluding commentary on managers' perspectives on decision processes:

- Strategic objectives for projects are seen as being highly desirable by IDV managers so that the role which they play in implementing the strategy is clearly specified.
- Decision criteria are, for both companies, a mix between strategic, financial and operational. The relative emphasis on each area varies between organisations, with IDV being apparently more concerned with financial criteria. Also decision criteria may vary according to the kind of project being considered.
- The 'cost of capital' emerges as being cloudy and hard to define. Doug Waddell of IDV feels strongly that there is a danger of going too far in seeking accurate and discriminating measures of cost of capital. There are also indications of uncertainty, in practice, of when to use which tool, although Simon Hart later points out that, with medium-term projects, payback can be used as a surrogate for IRR. IDV is attached to IRR partly because of its simplicity. Both organisations cite cases where payback was used successfully to flush out high return project items or to reshape less attractive projects.
- Financial modelling is seen as an important and central tool by IDV. Although this is in use equally at Rolls Royce, managers at IDV balance the use of financial models against the perceived need to identify indicators which give early warnings of external discontinuity.
- The issue of the 'role of Directors' occurs specifically only for Rolls Royce where managers prefer to see them having an involvement which probes key assumptions rather than becoming immersed in fine detail assumptions.
- Prioritisation is seen as difficult to organise, as projects cannot be lined up simultaneously for comparison.
- Finally, financial constraints are believed to be influential in both cases. There are clear hints that systems of accounting-based,

short-term control are in tension with longer-term, economically based decision systems within the management process.

The final point is now reinforced in the next section on 'controls'.

CONTROLS

For both organisations controls emerge as major influences in the decision-making process. Controls thus shape the entire project formulation and evaluation process, even though actually they may be applied to the implementation end of that process.

For instance, Simon Hart reflects that:

> We do have [implicit] strategic controls. The day you decide to go and launch a new product, you not only decide to launch a new product but you also decide when this actually is going to start flying.

But Rolls Royce managers appear ambivalent to post audit-based controls. First, Simon Hart exposes scepticism of project audit controls, and second, Austin Brackin reflects on the tendency of controls to escalate in complexity:

> The fact that you spent that money is really history . . . sure, you can have a witch-hunt on how it did or did not go and rationalise it today, but . . . I agree, in the strategic sense it's absolutely vital to learn the lessons from investment which went wrong, but I suspect that the reality is that post audits are not as important as we like to think they are.
>
> (Simon Hart)

> A lot of these things are in danger of . . . you build in a damned great bureaucracy . . . you just bog yourself down in red tape which doesn't satisfy the need to do the job.
>
> (Austin Brackin)

This problem highlights that control systems themselves may involve, in effect, an investment in the decision process which invariably appears to yield incremental benefits. But these 'improvements' may also result in harder-to-define incremental costs. For example, controls may unduly slow down the decision-making process.

Turning to IDV, Doug Waddell also shows an interest in strategic controls in parallel with Rolls Royce. He says 'An area which he [the planner] hasn't yet got to grips with is how we are progressing against the strategy.'

And on other controls Doug Waddell identifies problems of *post appraisal* of acquisition performance:

> We do post audits of acquisitions; we tend to do this two years after. It is sometimes very difficult to evaluate when businesses merge. Initially it is possible to identify the elements, then you find this increasingly difficult as the business becomes split up. You need to ask 'were differences in performance due to the purchase or with management'?

David Shephard goes on to describe in greater detail the process of review for both acquisitions and organic investment projects:

> The manager knows that some time within the next two years, he's going to be held accountable for what he said, so it's just that he's probably going to give a more realistic view of the project.
> The post appraisal process is financially driven . . . we don't have . . . sharing of experience on how you integrate things.

Although IDV are *tight* on controls, managers are aware that the *focus* of controls may be narrower than what is ideal:

> There is nothing in that post-acquisition audit that says, you know, have the assumptions for the next ten years changed?

As a wider issue, both IDV managers highlight the importance of controls in guarding against over-optimistic investment plans:

> If they [proposed business cases] are not well controlled, people coming in with inflated sales projections or whatever, then that is a very important factor in central management deciding or not to hand resources to the management team.
>
> (Doug Waddell)

> There would be a provision in the plan which his bonus would be based on, so he would be penalised if he really screwed up.
>
> (David Shephard)

The financial control systems outlined above thus appear to be tightly geared up to IDV's rewards and recognition systems.

David Shephard (IDV) raises the problem of monitoring the performance for an opportunity with long-time horizons, indicating that whilst controls may be robust for shorter-term performance measurement, their effectiveness fades rapidly for longer-term investment:

> The sales projections are for five years – how do you know after you've set up a project; how can you actually review that project?

Finally, this issue should be addressed on the basis of managers' forecasting performance in the past, according to Dave Waddell (IDV) who says 'We should be good at pinning them [managers] down and ascertaining whether or not they are good at appraising projects.'

This shows how close the interrelationships are between managers' skills and related training requirements; the quality of reviews of investment cases and finally post-implementation reviews.

Commentary on managers' perspectives on controls:

- Both groups of managers are attracted to the idea of strategic controls either in explicit or implicit form.
- Rolls Royce managers are averse to adding undue bureaucracy into controls and Simon Hart, in particular, is sceptical of the value of post-implementation audits and reviews.
- Finally, IDV managers appear particularly keen on pinning managers down to the assumptions which they have made to ensure that they do not put optimistic gloss on proposals.

SUBJECTIVE JUDGEMENT

This short section covers subjective belief and fear (which links back to uncertainty). The issue of the role of subjective judgement is raised primarily by Rolls Royce. Initially Simon Hart discloses:

> Probably it is a criticism of the accountants that it is they who believe the assumptions, rather than worrying about the processing of the assumptions. Around the assumptions is a tremendous amount of subjectivity. For example, in the case of an acquisition, there is a lot of subjectivity about it. There's more objectivity about capital plant.

Austin Brackin is even more direct about the limitations of theory (referring to financial theory in particular):

> Oh yeah, the theory. You can apply the theory, take a textbook. You can apply the theory until you are blue in the face. At the end of the day you sit back and say 'does it make sense?'

His personal 'treatment' for this is distilled neatly as 'Again it comes back to having a total view of the whole scenario.' Both managers pursue this issue further and show how the need for subjective judgement is amplified when projects are clothed in layers of uncertainty:

> When it comes to project launch, finance come forward with a project yield, say nine point nine per cent which is say, below the threshold. All their

judgements would be brought to bear. I guess that all decisions (ultimately) end up as subjective decisions.

(Austin Brackin)

We seem to add uncertainty on uncertainty and I suppose that's why we find it more and more difficult. We have enough uncertainty with the variables and we seem to be adding a lot more uncertainty.

(Simon Hart)

Austin Brackin takes this a stage further and highlights the interaction of uncertainty, fear and subjective judgement in decision-making:

What you would do in our industry is, you would frighten yourself to death . . . If it created an atmosphere in which you were terrified of doing anything you would have created a worse situation than you've got at the moment. Some of the decisions, possible scenarios, are so imponderable that if you really, consciously set out to look at them, you would never, ever, take any decisions. So it is better to take some decisions in sheer ignorance.

Austin Brackin is very open here about the problems faced when deciding what areas of uncertainty to explore, and what other areas to be aware of peripherally.

By comparison, IDV managers are quiet on the topic of subjective judgement, although glimmers of this important ingredient in decision-making are revealed in David Shephards words:

Launching a new brand is very difficult and is very much an act of faith. On the other hand, you may have other measures, whether . . . of increasing market share.

Commentary on the last section

Subjective judgement emerges as an important ingredient in the decision-making process for Rolls Royce. At IDV it appears less crucial but shows itself to be at work in appraisal of new brands. What also surfaces is a strong undercurrent of fear which surrounds the making of major and, in part, irreversible, longer-term financial decisions where value is dependent upon a number of (external) uncertainties.

PRACTICAL LESSONS FROM THE CASE

Value of investment decisions

1. 'Longer-term financial decisions' are not merely capital but include non-capital areas of investment and also revenue costs involving longer-term time lag to recoup benefits.
2. Investment in a business may be apparently justified on the basis of 'incremental net benefits' whilst there may be adverse effect on the overall business. The investment may add to complexity of the business structure and inadvertently generate costs by distracting from the original strategic focus.
3. Country investment requires evaluation of a range of tangible and less tangible values – both determinate *and* contingent. The consequences of inadequate appraisal of the value of country strategy in financial terms may be that investment is misallocated to 'fashionable places to be in'.
4. The base case *is* inherently difficult to evaluate, especially where it is in decline and the pace of decline is hard to predict. But unless the impact of this decline is incorporated within assumptions, managers may need to 'pump up' their assumptions in order to justify investment where much of the value is to protect the existing business.
5. Protective value is an important channel through which value can be created. It is important to recognise this so that funding is not over-allocated to apparently attractive extensions of the business.
6. Intangible, contingent and opportunity value evaluation requires clear guidelines – if included in the appraisal these should cover how they are to be measured and controlled and, if excluded, then how are these to be 'weighed' in the aggregate against financial measures?
7. Valuing business strategy can be a powerful application of economic (financial) analysis. But unless the key assumptions which underpin these business strategies are recognised, the results will be at best illustrative. Likewise, terminal values are notional without full support of assumptions about the longer-term environment and competitive position.

Uncertainty and Interdependency

1. External analysis should be focused on *key sources of discontinuity* rather than primarily on extrapolation of trends.

2. Competitor analysis requires insightful and creative thinking rather than massive data gathering. In order to get managers 'hooked' on competitor analysis it needs to become a central part of their thinking about the business rather than being incorporated into 'yet another system' peripheral to the management process.

3. In most management environments risk and uncertainty analysis may be usefully explored using simple, pictorial displays rather than via complex, statistical methodologies.

4. Managers need to avoid the trap of raising the hurdle rate to accommodate project-specific risk.

5. Interdependencies are amenable to being *mapped*. This is the first stage in evaluating their potential impact. Managers may benefit from recognising that this opens up a debate as to how value is being created (and diluted or destroyed) within a complex business structure.

Decision processes

1. Setting strategic objectives for investment projects may:

   - help link those projects closely to the strategy;
   - identify more clearly how value is being created by those projects;
   - provide a means of sharpening up the business strategy and updating it to reflect external change (thus helping to avoid the periodic 'big bang' strategic review).

2. Managers may believe it is better to leave 'decision criteria' loose and fluid so that there is maximum scope for flexibility in decision-making. However, the anticipated consequences of this may be that decision-making appears inconsistent, tortuous and may also appear to use strategic, financial and operational criteria in an *ad hoc* fashion. This suggests merit in laying down explicit criteria for 'acceptable' longer-term financial decisions. These criteria can then be used as benchmarks in order to debate exceptions and borderline cases – but not as hard and fast 'hurdles'.

3. It is unwise to rely upon a single financial measure and managers are warned that IRR can (with certain cash flow profiles) produce misleading results. Also, if payback is to be used as a targeting device this might be best made explicit in the management process.

4. Managers need to remind themselves constantly that financial models *do not remove* fundamental uncertainties. Financial sensitivity analysis needs to be driven by analysis of business risks and uncertainties,

not by arbitrary changes in the value of particular variables. One suggestion is to surface all these risks and uncertainties *before* playing with the financial model. But this requires a shift in management's appraisal style so that they can accept more 'uncertainty discomfort' in the range of financial outcomes which are possible.

5. How (and when) the directors and senior managers will add value to the decision process needs to be explicitly defined.

6. As projects do not often line up neatly at the same instant in time, it may be necessary to refer back explicitly to past (similar) projects in the business case. This should be a feasible option where these projects are subjected to ongoing monitoring.

7. The issue of conflict between economic bases of decision-making and the apparent constraint of maintaining target growth in reported earnings (measured on an accounting basis) needs to be explicitly addressed. First, managers need to test whether, and to what extent, this is a real constraint or whether shareholders can be 'sold' the longer-term benefits of particular programmes. Second, if there is a perceived constraint then the extent to which resources are shifted into short-term payback projects should be carefully evaluated, and particularly to highlight the longer-term economic costs. Also, the effect on competitive advantage needs to be addressed, particularly where the company competes in Europe, globally or against imports into the UK.

Controls

1. Appraisal targets and measures need to be aligned both to controls and rewards and recognition systems to have maximum effect.

2. This alignment is particularly difficult for externally facing or longer-term measures of performance (ie 'strategic controls'), or where value is of a less tangible nature. Where value is softer, or where what is being measured is inherently hard to define, this invites the use of broadly-defined, rather than precisely-defined, control measures. Managers are advised, however, that this may put additional strain of interpretation on them when judging performance. This is a feature which managers in companies who operate in primarily a financial control style may find extremely difficult.

Subjective judgement

1. Subjective judgement is a valuable ingredient in the decision process

but it should not be used as a substitute for strategic and financial analysis.

2. To apply strategic analysis thoroughly this may involve surfacing and examining major (uncomfortable) uncertainties. These may be very fear-provoking for senior managers who need to avoid repressing those assumptions which are 'most uncertain and high-potential impact' – often the latter may never get onto the appraisal agenda at all.

CONCLUSIONS

Here we examine the question raised in the introduction and attempt to answer this. First, let us turn to the problems caused by managers making implicit, as opposed to explicit, linkages of strategic and financial appraisal.

The resulting problems appear to be as follows:

- Brands appear difficult to evaluate, not only financially but also strategically.
- Investment in country position, protective areas of value, opportunity and contingent value and terminal value are inherently hard to quantify with precision.
- There are also major problems associated with a number of areas of value defined as 'intangibles'.
- The above problems are compounded by both external and internal uncertainty and interdependency, and more specifically by the problem of hard-to-evaluate competitor intent. Conventional risk analysis seems to be unable to cope with these major complexities underlying decisions.
- There are also major difficulties purely of a decision process nature. This includes deciding what decision criteria to apply and where; in determining appropriate financial measures; and finally in reconciling differing priorities and financial constraints.
- There are also other very important issues of aligning the appraisal process with reward and control systems and also in determining how best to blend subjective judgement with more objective, analytical thinking in the decision process.

Of the above problems, perhaps the 'easiest' turn out to be essentially technical in nature. For instance, the definition of 'cost of capital' is, perhaps, mainly a technical issue which can be resolved through appropriate routines. The major problems above, therefore, appear to involve the use of less clear-cut and intuitive thinking, which one might call 'soft value analysis'. Leading on from this, control measures might also be broadened to include controls of a 'soft' or indicative kind rather than being exact and highly specific. These arguments are taken up in Chapter 9.

To conclude, the Rolls Royce Aeroengines and IDV cases highlight the following facts relating to investment decisions:

- 'Longer-term financial decisions' cover not merely capital investment but a whole range of thrusts, many of which are recorded as revenue costs (including brand investment).
- The financial value of these decisions may be best understood often not by seeing investment projects as stand-alone but by understanding first how they contribute to an outward-facing strategy.
- Once this role is clarified the next step in injecting vision into the valuation process is to explore fully the fundamental external uncertainties and interdependencies which act as key value drivers. This may require difficult and sometimes uncomfortable analysis of possible futures which may suggest that the value of these strategies is vulnerable.
- Only then should more detailed financial modelling of internal assumptions and interdependencies be performed.
- These steps may require considerable overhaul of the decision process and underlying systems and style of appraisal.

7

CASE ON INVESTMENT DECISIONS - LONDON UNDERGROUND AND POST OFFICE COUNTERS LIMITED

INTRODUCTION

This case contains managers' perspectives on investment decisions from both London Underground and Post Office Counters Limited. This joint case again highlights key similarities and differences – this time for two public sector businesses. The case is set out as follows:

- Background to the case
- Value of investment decisions
- Uncertainty and interdependency
- Decision processes
- Controls
- Subjective judgement
- Practical lessons from the case
- Conclusions.

BACKGROUND TO THE CASE

London Underground Limited (LUL) is a part of London Regional Transport (LRT) and has the responsibility of operating and improving the existing tube network in London. It does not have responsibility for constructing new tube lines. Nevertheless, it is responsible for investing almost £400 million per annum, which, according to much press comment following the 1991 publication of a Monopolies and Mergers Commission report, ought to be at least £700 million per annum. A prevalent view, both publicly and within London Underground is that it has suffered years of neglect and underinvestment, despite current levels of funding. In 1991 the Government authorised annual investment rising to over £1 billion. The two managers involved in this case are John Vaughan, Investment Controller, and Peter Clark, Manager, Capital Appraisal.

London Underground invests in a number of areas including new rolling stock, refurbishment of existing stock, station modernisation, property, communication and other systems, and escalators.

Post Office Counters Limited is a business within the Post Office. It is responsible for running a network of over 20,000 post office counters in the UK. It serves a number of external clients including the Department of Social Security (DSS), Girobank and DVL and has a very wide customer base. Its principal business activities include administration, the physical transmission of cash, premises development and subsidiary retail activities. Although it invests a much smaller amount than London Underground this is compensated for by the difficulties of appraising its investment programme.

The managers involved from Post Office Counters Limited (POCL) in this research were David Marshall, Management Accountant, responsible for management accounting and Andy Cook, Head of Corporate Planning and Investment Appraisal, assistant to David Marshall (and subsequently Geoff Fletcher).

Again it may be useful for the reader to reflect on the following question: '*To what extent are London Underground and Post Office Counters' problems of appraisal caused by a lack of explicit linkages of strategic and financial appraisal?*'

VALUE OF INVESTMENT DECISIONS

This initial section focuses on financial measurement of the 'worth' of investment decisions. Subsequent sections deal with the additional problems posed by uncertainty and interdependency.

The key areas explored by managers on value include the impact of investment decisions; replacement and refurbishment; automation; image; safety and security; protective value and the base case; customer value; intangibles; value of the strategy.

Impact of investment decisions

David Marshall (POCL) reflects on decision types that 'investment' does not equate purely with 'capital':

One thing was the question of what actually constitutes a project. We tend to say things which are 'capital' are projects and we religiously say that, all the time it is non-recurring revenue. But I actually think that there is a lot of expenditure in the organisation that we don't look at in quite the way that we should.

Replacement and refurbishment

First, David Marshall positions refurbishment as an area of investment with strategic implications. He states that 'Certainly things like refurbishment are strategic. In our case, it is creating a look for the company.'

John Vaughan (LUL) also explores the need to look at options in a wider context when considering replacement:

> An example of that (replacement) would be ECTV (close-circuit TV) where we have lots of little packages where you would get one global CCTV . . . It might be better to buy a bigger, multi-purpose network which will serve lots of individuals rather than each have a stand-alone system. The thing is moving that way. Let's buy something bigger than we need for this project, because the spare capacity can come along handy later.

This is echoed by Andy Cook (POCL) who tells the story of how options for refurbishment evolved:

> We decided we were going for a certain type of refurbishment which is pretty expensive without really knowing whether that was the most cost effective way of dealing with it. Subsequently we decided it wasn't because we decided to do some basic, cheaper type of scheme and our internal market research indicated that [the benefits of the more expensive scheme] made little difference.

He goes on to say:

> We've got such a diversity of locations. We may have two offices that are roughly the same size but with completely different types of business and you may want to do something completely different to attract customers.

David Marshall then reflects on the problem:

> Do we spend £200,000 doing a really good tart-up [of the offices] or do we spend £25,000 or £50,000? If we've got to bring them all up to a very high standard, the answer is, we can't justify it. So we actually come down and down to the point where really all you do is to paint them.

This situation is in sharp contrast with LUL where managers built up the definition of the project to embrace a concept with wider value-adding potential. Here at POCL it becomes difficult to justify major investment on refurbishment, so the approach of building up from minimalist levels of investment is adopted.

Automation

Automation is a major area in Post Office Counters' investment programme. Ideas on how to approach this opportunity have evolved considerably over a number of years. David Marshall (POCL) tells us:

> We had a classic example of an iterative process. As well as full counters automation, we are also thinking of introducing electronic cash registers as a means of improving accuracy and cost reduction. In the first trial we did we found that the time taken in serving customers had gone up by 10 per cent. Initially we felt that was wrong. So although it went to the Board saying, there wasn't a financial case, there was a recommendation that we should try it again. We did further sampling after six months and found that there was a very long learning curve for the counter clerks. So what we have done is to implement a much tighter training scheme.
>
> We also insisted that we spend more money on the facilities for electronic cash registers so that eventually we would be able to upgrade the machinery that we put in under that scheme, to fit in with full automation.

The above example of automation highlights how the appraisal process can be moulded by a number of factors, including the fluid definition of the project and its underlying objectives, the perceived need for flexibility and also pressure to conserve scarce investment funds.

Image

London Underground managers face problems in justifying how much and what to spend on image development. John Vaughan reflects that:

> British Rail's Network South-East, red lamp-post land, was about image. That investment was to make people think that things were happening. They were, but that wasn't seen.

This is echoed by David Marshall (POCL):

> We have been trying to look at what value people put on image. Image-building schemes tend not to give a payback because we don't perhaps value them in quite the way that London Underground do.

Image, perhaps, represents a most difficult area to evaluate yet companies often spend millions of pounds on it (for example, in changing ICI's and BT's logos). Image would appear to be an area which is heavily dependent on a number of variables. These include achieving shifts in external perception of an organisation, which in turn is interdependent with that organisation's market posture, its ability to deliver to customers and also to its positioning relative to competitors.

Safety and security

Both LUL managers surface 'safety' as a key issue. John Vaughan explains:

> Coming back to our safety case, would you say that our sort of approach was quite legitimate? If you decide that you have to do something on safety grounds, all sorts of things which you never quite justify doing on their own become OK because there is only a marginal cost.

Peter Clark (LUL) comments on this problem and compares it with the insurance industry:

> The benefit of the insurance thing is that they have a million deaths every year, so they know exactly the probability of your going to drop dead next week.

This poses major difficulties for managers for which conventional statistical approaches appear unsuited. Peter Clark expands:

> When you are looking at an accident, you may have one in fifty years, whereas the consequences are horrendous, the probability of 0.0001 times £100 million comes to three pounds, but what does it mean?

Turning to Post Office Counters, David Marshall then raises the issue of appraising security investment both relative to the costs of losses and also relative to external benchmarks:

> The other area is, how much do we spend on security? At the moment we spend as much each year on security as we lose, in terms of losses throughout the business. Now is that right? Is that good? I don't know.

He also reflects on a meeting with managers from Securicor to share approaches to security investment that:

> I think that their [Securicor's] general line was that their whole existence is security, therefore they cannot really afford to have a major attack, a major successful attack. Therefore they pumped money into security in a way that I guess we couldn't afford to do.

The problem becomes very much one of deciding a cut-off point for investment. David Marshall continues:

> The area that was running through my mind was cash centres and the difficulty which you have there is knowing how much to spend on them, on each individual site. You should really take every possible conceivable

– er – precaution to make sure that no one takes all that money. There is also, in terms of assessing the likelihood of the attack, the need to take account of whether they [the criminals] know where the centre is. If it is in a totally green field area, then the likelihood of attack is probably greater than if you build it alongside a Payless DIY. And the concept of trying to put values on all of those things is very difficult.

Post Office Counters are not alone in this. Peter Clark of LUL remarks on security of passengers in the Underground:

> People's expectations have changed, not just in the Underground areas . . . It is strategic, the world has changed and people are threatened on the Underground.

Safety and security emerge as being very important but very difficult areas to appraise because of the difficulties of predicting (relatively) unlikely and infrequent events. But just as we see later on that London Underground's concept of 'degrees of (competitive) advantage' may be of help, perhaps this suggests the ability of 'degrees of protection'. In the latter case there may be diminishing returns to investment spend. Or, there may be cases where two or more projects may reinforce each other to provide protective synergies. Also, there may be alternative mixes of investment and change in operating routines which may be used to achieve the same strategic objective.

Protective value and the base case

Both London Underground and Post Office Counters face major problems in renewal of existing businesses in order to improve and even simply to protect existing service standards. Post Office Counters give the most in depth account of this as follows. This links the need for investment with the strategy of the business and also with problems of the financial measurement of incremental cash flows where, on a 'without investment' basis (or 'base case'), projected net cash flows may decline.

David Marshall also raises issues relating to *protective investment* to ward off decline, and then reflects on how this links to *decision criteria*:

> The Post Office is essentially there to provide the kind of things that the private sector can't provide. If you follow that attitude, then you get into horrendous problems. What you end up by saying is, well, the only thing that's open to the counters business is decline, and then consider the most efficient way of managing that decline. So you don't spend any money on automation because it's not going to be a solution with a fast payback, you don't spend any money on refurbishment to any great extent, because why do that?

This situation was reflected in a 'declining base case' scenario for Post Office Counters automation investment:

> Our classic example [of the base case] is counters automation. If you don't automate, what happens? I'm bound to say that the justification for counters automation was very much a base case led justification. It wasn't as if there were going to be lots of good things that you think would come out of it . . . but it is very difficult to forecast what that base case is actually going to be.

Although managers here made use of the concept of a declining base case, the comments from these managers suggest that they are still areas of discomfort, particularly when it comes down to specifying the likely impact on financial projections.

Customer value

As investment projects aim ultimately to provide a service in both organisations, the issue of links between *customer value* and *business investment* appears important. John Vaughan (LUL):

> I think we were saying that an awful lot of our expenditure wasn't seen by the passenger and therefore may not be valued by them, and we actually might need to highlight the things which we did see. We may need to do some things disproportionately to be seen.

Both 'perceived' and 'real' customer benefits which are the target of London Underground's investment programme also link in to LUL's pricing policy:

> We need to aggregate these [passenger benefits] because we ought to find a way eventually, if we are continually improving what passengers are getting for their money, we should be able to raise that backbone of fares.

There are some remarkably close parallels here with Post Office Counters. David Marshall (POCL) reveals that a lot of analysis is done of customers' perceptions of value as input to financial evaluation:

> We do a lot of market research and some funny messages arise. If people wait, say, for three minutes, they think they have got good service. If they wait for three to five minutes, then something happens in their minds. They think they have waited a lot longer than three minutes.

But in contrast, he reflects on the conflict between pleasing customers and keeping costs low (the latter being in the interest of POCL's clients) that:

> Obviously customers like to have a nice environment, they like to watch

videos when they go in, they like to feel secure, they like to feel comfortable. On the other hand, the people who actually pay out, our clients, have a whole range of different desires, some of them want really just a warehouse, or against that you've got other people who are very much in competition in the marketplace who want a completely different set of environmental factors in the office.

The complex nature of Post Office Counters' business scope and strategy thus makes it hard to focus on investment plans on adding value to specific target areas of demand.

Finally, John Vaughan (LUL) reveals a further difficulty relating to measurement and control systems of customer benefits for London Underground:

The line manager said, well I would actually not rather have this extra staircase for the benefit of passengers, I would rather have the extra site revenue which I would get from the developer. In other words [laughing], to hell with the notional gold, give me the real gold – because he doesn't see the notional gold affected anywhere in his performance statistics. In other words, we will give you projects which have a passenger benefit but only to the extent that you could encash that benefit by raising the fares.

Finally John Vaughan (LUL) reflects on linkages between customer value, pricing policy and LUL's mission:

The idea [behind the new 'mission' statement] is to make it [the Underground] a better, a more pleasant environment, what have you. I think we would be trying to move into an area where we would be prepared to pay a bit more than is really necessary and plough that money rather more into investment.

Customer value is thus an important factor in the thinking of both London Underground and Post Office Counters. But there are some difficult issues emerging here: where additional customer value is created, to what extent is this shared by the customer versus the supplier: indeed in these public sector contexts, the issue arises as to what extent it should be harvested by the customer (as value he is 'entitled to') without payment, versus it being captured by the organisation in price increases.

Intangibles

Both organisations spend a lot of effort in understanding intangibles. Beginning with London Underground, John Vaughan reveals a useful idea of 'degrees of advantage':

The other useful thing is, you get to the stage where you look at something you are able to afford. You do so in *degrees of advantage* until you spend the money that is available at an accepted cost. You can work out an improvement to a station, look at what that will yield and say, right, the pass mark means we can spend up to so much.

Peter Clark (LUL) also highlights the need to have some ultimate measures of these intangible benefits:

> We have a lot of space-saving projects. You cannot say that you are going to stop leasing a building but you can say that, if you keep doing this, we shall stop. It is going to come sometime, it must be of benefit to the company.

John Vaughan (LUL) applies this concept specifically to investment in training:

> We look at our level of training, a new training centre, a much more efficient training system, we can cut out our wastage rates by 10 per cent and we can also reduce the failure rate of new entrants by about 10 per cent which means that the better training will have a pay-off, we can actually do an appraisal. The assumptions can be tested.

Evaluating intangibles is not, however, plain sailing. Andy Cook (POCL) explains his concerns:

> Our strategy is to make the most of return, at the same time as doing all sorts of other things which don't show a return, which are seen as being very important to us, like security. But how do you position those things that don't make a return, things like security which you can't quantify?

But David Marshall (POCL) provides a useful hint on how to deal with intangibles – to sort these into generic categories which then enable assessment tools to be developed, tailored to each:

> There has been a tendency in our people to throw up lots of advantages whilst the basic thrust of the project may vary, the intangibles that are being thrown up actually don't.

So-called 'intangibles' thus form an important ingredient in the decision-making process in both companies – and represents value which they explicitly incorporate (in financial terms) in the decision-making process.

Value of the strategy

In common with Rolls Royce in Chapter 6, Post Office Counters managers show a keen interest in the *value of strategy*. David Marshall begins:

They are running that through their computer. The way to look at it is to say, if we get 90 per cent of the projects which fulfil business strategy x, what does that do to the NPV of the plan as a whole? What would we be prepared to pay for the strategy?

Andy Cook flags up some problems which have arisen in developing a process for evaluation. This appears to suggest either that managers are looking for answers of a too precise nature, or that they have not yet evolved a sufficiently robust framework for qualitative and quantitative analysis of areas of intangibles. He says 'At the moment we can ask the question "are we willing to pay that?" but we haven't really got any ideas what it is worth.'

In the above case the team working on valuing the business strategy is separate from Counters business financial managers, which may have contributed to the difficulty in implementing change.

Commentary on value

- In parallel with the Chapter 6 cases, it was recognised that 'investment' represents longer-term financial commitment in areas beyond 'capital investment'.
- When managers examined it closely, the issue of what to appraise became ambiguous. Although they had traditionally defined the 'unit of appraisal' in physical terms or through area of functional responsibility, closer analysis revealed broader linkages between different but related areas of investment. This also led into an appreciation that there may well be other options to the early definition of the project.
- Both companies shared difficulties in deciding how much to invest in specific areas such as image-building, safety and security. Their approaches to appraising these areas seemed to be conditioned by a broader concept of what the business should be investing in, its attitude to risk and its self image generally (its 'investment paradigm'.
- Post Office Counters' managers in particular had previously employed base case analysis built on assumptions of decline, but this had not appeared to trigger fundamental strategic questions about how that decline could be influenced.
- Both companies appeared to be receptive and proactive in evaluating less tangible areas of value including 'customer value'. An interesting insight was that 'intangibles' might be amenable to analysis rather than seen as 'the black box' of unquantified value.

UNCERTAINTY AND INTERDEPENDENCY

This section covers external uncertainty, political influences and government, risk and internal interdependency.

External uncertainty

Peter Clark (LUL) perceives that stability acts to *reduce* external uncertainty because 'Passengers will keep on getting on and off, travelling and paying money.' Peter Clark further reflects that competitive rivalry for LUL's services is not fierce: 'We are not really competing against the private sector.'

Referring to London Buses, John Vaughan of LUL adds 'Yes, we don't dwell much on competition do we? We have them, but they belong to the same company.'

This lack of intense competitive pressure may be a factor inhibiting the perceived need to link strategic and financial appraisal. In particular it clouds the issue of to what extent improvements in service should be harvested as price increases making it more difficult to benchmark this variable against either competitors or close parallels.

David Marshall (POCL) points out a more intense set of competitive pressure, although this has some limits:

> There is a difference of opinion as to whether we are in a competitive environment or not. If you look at our core business, then yes we are in a competitive environment in the sense that the banks can offer a lot of these services. But it is not as competitive as Menzies or Smiths. If I have a pension I cannot just go to the bank to get my money. There is a difference.

Paradoxically, the lack of clear sources of intense competition across the board may therefore make it *more difficult* to justify investment by both London Underground and the Post Office in improving services. This deficit may be made up by the indirect route of Government and political pressure or by customer pressure groups, or simply by pressure from top management within London Underground (as in their 1991 'Company Plan').

Political influences and government

A major issue which is surfaced by both LUL managers is *political influences and government*. Peter Clark begins by saying 'There are a lot of ideas, the high fare scenario, the low fare scenario, high investment scenario. A whole matrix of these things.'John Vaughan (LUL) illustrates this:

> For example, in a recent project to relieve passenger congestion, if fares are not increased, the passenger benefits will be this, if fares are increased then the benefits will be less. These things do get taken into account but that's not always terribly easy.
>
> Just this week or so, the fares policy makes a lot of difference, a fares policy and two per cent compound growth means the difference between finding a new tube line is to be built and no tube line being built.

Major constraints are also perceived by POCL as affecting the scope and type of business activity which POCL may invest in:

> We are able to use surplus space and we put things like photo booths in, also film processing. What we are not able to do is to decide, if we don't need a post office, to exploit that in other ways.
>
> There are a lot of things which we could do within the market place with full automation, but then the question is, can we justify expenditure at some basic level of automation that allows the same sort of cost reduction?

Not surprisingly, therefore, political influences and government represent a major uncertainty, perhaps equivalent to the external competitive uncertainty which the earlier private sector companies faced.

Risk assessment

John Vaughan of LUL highlights the problems of evaluating risk when he says 'The bean counter says at the same time, here's all your figures, but its terribly grey because there is so much uncertainty.' David Marshall (POCL) also experiences difficulties both conceptual and also cultural:

> We also undertake risk analysis, in the sense that we assign reasonable risk to variables. We throw them into the black box. The likelihood is this one becoming more and more a valuable part of the process. There's more to do on that.
>
> We've gone quite a long way in terms of analysing risk, the problem then is, once you've got to that stage what are people's attitudes to it? You know, there is a tendency to be risk averse.

Attitudes to risk appear to be very important in underpinning analysis at Post Office Counters Limited:

> If there is ever a chance of someone being killed by a robbery, then you go all out to avoid that and it costs you a fortune and you do create a lot of problems for yourselves with the people who you are trying to communicate with.

Internal interdependency

John Vaughan (LUL) then reflects on the importance of *internal interdependency* and appears to conclude that there are alternatives to past ways of defining the unit of analysis, based on an understanding of interdependencies:

> Yes we did look at them [the projects] individually, I don't think we looked at them in total.
>
> If someone stood back and said, with all these small bits, isn't there an opportunity to do something where the overall is vastly greater than the sum of these small bits.

Andy Cook (POCL) echoes this by identifying *internal interdependency* between areas of investment:

> One of the things that we have dealt with is to look at these things in the overall, strategic context. Having said that, I'm not sure that it is sufficiently clear in terms of the linkage say, between refurbishment and automation etc, how that all fits together as a business case, that's difficult.

David Marshall also recalls past investment programmes and on the definition of the investment programme via specific, discrete projects:

> It is not a consistent approach. We have some things which we have done well and then there is a tatty old writing desk there. We ought to do the security and everything else all at one go. It doesn't strike me as particularly difficult. Alright you have got to co-ordinate a number of people.

He also highlights the consequences that might occur:

> You can say, well, here's a refurbishment. If you are digging up the road, you can dig it up as often as you like, for electricity or for gas. We ought to be saying 'the project' is the building or the branch . . . we don't do that, we do dig up the road several times.

David Marshall also links the 'definition of business we are in' with the process of value creation through closely interdependent areas of investment – ' . . . You go down the retail route as well as the core route because you are using the same investment for that again.'

On a similar note, John Vaughan of London Underground concludes:

> Whilst you are going to do one thing, aren't there other things which . . . whilst doing that we can refurbish them, and do all of these things without the loss of revenues.

Perhaps more than the earlier cases on Rolls Royce and IDV, this illustrates the degree to which apparently 'fixed' definitions of projects and investment programmes can be resegmented. This can be done in ways which shed new light on how value is created through the interaction of different elements in the strategy.

Commentary

This section on uncertainty and interdependency highlights the following factors:

- For both these public sector organisations the primary source of uncertainty is perceived as being Government-influenced, rather than competitive pressure specifically. However, in London Underground's case it is possible that customer militancy could be an increasingly important but uncertain factor. Also, for Post Office Counters some components of existing business might well be vulnerable to pressure.
- Both sets of managers also focus on internal interdependencies and risks rather than (particularly) external interdependencies. This contrasts somewhat with both the Rolls Royce and IDV cases earlier.

DECISION PROCESSES

This section deals with the management processes involved in evaluating strategic investment decisions. It covers a number of areas including strategic decisions; definition of the strategy; strategic objectives; business plans; decision criteria; the cost of capital; prioritisation; financial constraints; role of directors; and finally, marginal analysis.

Strategic decisions

Both Post Office Counters managers raise issues concerning the making of *strategic decisions*, including the source of ideas and generation of options for investment. Andy Cook begins:

> When you go back to the sourcing of ideas for projects, a lot of the capital planning is generated from the bottom-up, whereas the actual strategy is, as far as I am aware, one of top-down.

Whilst earlier in this book (Chapter Five), it was emphasised that strategy often emerged through individual decision-making, in practice it would appear from the above that this may result in problems of proliferation of investment projects unless there is some underlying top-down 'strategic glue' available.

David Marshall (POCL) also adds:

> We insist that people look at options, but the options that you may get are totally unrealistic, and they are only there because somebody said there must be some options in there. If there aren't then I would rather that somebody said, we've looked at it, and explain why, rather than create something which is a non-starter, or unrealistic.

Not all decisions, therefore, need to be given the treatment of screening for strategic fit and 'best available strategic option', where these revolve around filling a clear and simple operational need. However, caution is advised here as sometimes replacement decisions can overlook the existence of far more powerful technological approaches.

Indeed the idea of what 'strategic decisions' include is not always self-evident. For instance, at London Underground, John Vaughan says:

> We tend to classify as strategic projects where we are moving into new areas. These sorts of decisions have tended to be called *strategic.*

This suggests that major investment decisions within existing business scope are not described typically as strategic even though they represent major, long-term financial commitments. The label of strategic itself does seem to be one which is potentially dangerous and following up Rolls Royce's concerns that strategic means 'an excuse for financial failure' it would appear that it is often used as a convenient label to justify a decision.

Definition of the strategy

John Vaughan of London Underground comments on some external influences which shape 'the strategy':

> You are investing for ten, twenty, thirty, forty years, assets against a political horizon which has potentially a maximum of five years – our objective has totally changed over the last ten years. Yet we have a long-term view but at the end of the day that strategy is thrown, or at least temporarily thrown off course.

Sometimes the strategy can also be changed more rapidly by external events than major strategic decisions can be made, let alone implemented, as John Vaughan (LUL) observes:

> We have the same sort of thing where power stations are coming to expiry. We were heading down that path when gas prices fell, and own-generation

became a very much more profitable thing. We had just had the King's Cross fire so rather than go back into own-generation, the message was, concentrate on your own business and don't do peripheral things unless they are absolutely essential. Well, we are now looking at other options. So the strategy has shifted three times, all in the space of just one project.

London Underground highlight some substantial difficulties in defining strategy:

Fares policy . . . if this is going to be our strategy it will be that we have strategic double vision, and this week we seem to be somewhere in the middle. I don't know how I can forecast for that.

This situation is closely paralleled by Post Office Counters. David Marshall tells us 'I don't think we've ever really looked at ourselves in the past in a particularly strategic manner, put it that way.' Having said that, Post Office Counters managers quickly begin to appreciate that many of the problems encountered when applying financial appraisal are related largely to this absence of strategic thinking in the past. Areas where financial analysis appears to crumble are where hard value meets the edge of uncertainty, interdependency, ambiguity of definition in the base case and fuzzy definition of intangibles.

Strategic objectives

Strategic objectives appear to crystallise during the research as a way of linking strategic and financial appraisal. John Vaughan (LUL) reflects:

I think in our submissions we ought to say, this project is about cost savings, this project is about improved customer perception. We ought to do that.

What we are trying to do at the moment is to try and relate our present objectives against the strategy to highlight a) this is a desirable thing to do, but b) this is difficult at the moment because the strategy . . . the strategic objectives are terribly global.

This is a parallel issue for Post Office Counters. David Marshall contemplates a similar issue, highlighting the need *a)* to have a clear and detailed enough strategy in place and *b)* for this to be communicated to managers appraising major investment projects:

It may actually be easier to try and relate projects back to the mission statement than to relate them back to the business plan because of the problems with the business plan that I referred to earlier.

It is all very well saying projects have to fit with strategy, but strategy has to be known certainly by my team in some detail so that you can then assign things or otherwise.

Finally, London Underground experimented with the use of pictures to represent the strategic and financial characteristics of their large investment programme. John Vaughan (LUL) describes this:

> It might be worth mentioning very briefly that we used graphics a lot more this year. The interesting thing was, we went on to sell this to the civil servants, they could see the areas of colour. And it is an interesting concept because selling a capital programme on the basis of what you see rather than on the basis of what you can add up is not the way we have worked before.

This account of strategic objectives offers a positive guide to how greater vision can be injected into the appraisal process – nevertheless managers still required some convincing initially that this was worthwhile.

Business plans

David Marshall describes the fit he sees between business plans and the investment appraisal process, and goes on to evaluate why the planning processes are fragmented:

> The way I would like to see it work is that we have a business plan which is actually driving the business, far more than it does at the moment, and then we pick up the vibes from that, and we say 'this is what the business is seeking to do, we need you to develop the project within that.
>
> We've got a plan, then we go off and do the budget, the investment programme, but actually when people are thinking of schemes which they are wanting to spend money on, they don't look at that in the context of the plan.

Finally, he reflects on the potential value of forging much closer linkages between business and investment planning processes:

> We only do it in an isolated sense. We can't look at it in an overall business perspective, and therefore use the lessons to force down the business planning side. To get more realism into that [the business planning side] will take some time.

But Andy Cook reveals one possible *blocking* area to making closer linkages between strategic and financial appraisal within business plans as:

> There are more people involved who are close to what is being done, for example, at local level. The business plan is at a higher level, it has a bit of mystique.

One of the consequences of fragmentation of planning processes is that the links between strategic and financial appraisal and *operational* appraisal can become broken:

> We review it from a financial viewpoint, the operators say, yes, it's achievable, that goes ahead, then another one comes along. They don't relate the fact that they are perhaps using the same resources for project 2 as for project 1. It's that overall link which is missing.

The above highlights the ease with which separately defined planning processes and systems fragment. With a complex investment programme this can lead not just to multiple strategic vision but also to implementation difficulties. This fragmentation requires extensive effort to remedy as the amount of work by Post Office Counters managers since 1989 (when data was collected) to forge closer linkages bears testimony to.

Decision criteria

David Marshall (POCL) now links definition of strategy to the implicit idea of critical mass which may sometimes appear to conflict with financial measures:

> People say, 'what about project A? – it may give us a return', so we go for it. And I think we tend to spread ourselves a bit too thinly because of that.

David Marshall also says that internal resources can be inflexible – this factor may shape the allocation of investment resources:

> We are paying people to come up with these ideas, at some point in the future we have got to pump investment money, otherwise why bother to pay these people.

He then reflects on how certain investment projects were turned down in the past and links this to managers' aversion to risk. He also highlights that *decision criteria* are often implicit rather than explicit in the decision process:

> I feel that I am in two minds, five or six minds on this. We do have some quite interesting projects that come along . . . someone had the glimmer of an idea and it was developed very fast. It would be very interesting to analyse then why that did not go ahead.
>
> Now was that because actually the financials didn't stand up or was it that because they didn't, people saw that it didn't fit in with the strategy, the mission of the business? Or was it because, somehow, the Post Office got the feeling that it was a bit too new, a bit too 'leading edge', and we are not into these products. This is bearing in mind some of our experiences in the

past. Or was it a combination of these things and other factors as well?

I don't think it was purely a case of the financials not standing up. It was probably risk-averse forecasting and of course, at the end of the day, it was a big investment as well.

The above highlights the complex interaction of financial appraisal, the fit with strategy, the underlying comfort levels in the organisation to particular kinds of investment and managers' attitudes to risk.

Finally, an interesting shift in decision criteria is also noted by David Marshall, emphasising the need for a coherent vision in the decision making process:

I would still characterise the process as a bit of a hit-and-miss affair where, rather than say these are the areas we want you to come up with, projects with a good return, we see people scratching around for anything which will make a return. Because our process is driven by projects which will make a return we do invest in rather diverse things. I think we should concentrate more on developing projects which drive things together.

This section shows that managers found it difficult to create and apply clear and specific decision criteria and this problem appears to be greatly aggravated where there is some lack of clarity in the overall strategy. Looking back in 1992, David Marshall says:

. . . Counters has made considerable strides in the two areas of linking capital and overall strategic planning and tying down what have traditionally been seen as non-quantifiable benefits. The first of these has been achieved by much better process control throughout the strategic and business planning cycle . . . The second has been addressed by the . . . relative importance of the business' strategic aims . . . assessed by taking judgements from senior management. Second, the extent to which projects improve the business' performance has become a feature of project submissions . . . in effect a 'strategic concurrence for all major projects.'

The cost of capital

David Marshall of Post Office Counters Limited draws attention to the cost of capital definition as another issue:

We use a discount rate of 12 per cent which is supposed to represent the equivalent return in the private sector for a company operating without constraint.

The cost of capital appeared to be somewhat less contentious for both public sector companies than for the earlier private sector cases. Besides this input by Post Office Counters, London Underground managers' main comments were to the effect that they were reassured that the other three companies used an apparently similar rate to their own.

Prioritisation

Peter Clark describes plans to develop London Underground's prioritisation processes as:

> We are talking about prioritising our investment programme on a fairly formal basis, by benefits, costs, and we were constructing a database system which would do a lot of things . . .

John Vaughan adds:

> If we had to cut projects, we would rank them on that basis and we would start looking at all the things which were discretionary. We would rank these, those essential, and safety items would go straight through.

David Marshall reinforces earlier suggestions that prioritisation is perceived to be biased towards existing business areas:

> When we came around to doing the budget this time people said, well, we ought to be looking at the developments on smart cards, for example, but we weren't able to do that because people didn't see that as high priority. But if we look forward another 10 years to the ways in which money is going to be pushed around the economy; if we are going to be in the market place, we ought to be developing in the same way that the banks are developing.

David Marshall also describes the goal targeting system which now drives Post Office Counters' business plan and which will be used to prioritise projects:

> The goals are basically our business strategies, for example cost reduction or service. And we are trying to say what value would we actually put on those strategies in terms of financial value and NPV. This unfortunately has to be arbitrary in one sense. The value of the different strategies has to relate to one another as far as possible.

Although both companies are aware of the problems posed by prioritisation for a large (LUL) or complex (Post Office Counters) investment programme, this issue appears to be far more difficult in practice than is suggested by financial textbooks. This is perhaps because prioritisation is a complex organisational process and therefore analysis measures are not purely 'objective' but are highly charged, interpreted and reinterpreted at a number of levels. Here we therefore have two complex learning processes superimposed: first analytical learning and second interpersonal and process-related learning.

Financial constraints

David Marshall (POCL) appears to be in two minds on financial constraints:

> We tend to say, well, capital is constrained, but in fact, if I look back at the last four or five years then we have never had to spend up to our capital limit. Therefore, in that sense, it is something else that is constrained.
>
> We have external financing limit, that's a general target set by the Government; Corporate Group comes along and looks at the individual components of that target, and says, because capital is a component of that, then because the Corporation isn't meeting its EFL (external financing limit), the business has got to do something about it.

He then highlights the impact of shorter-term financial constraints:

> Whilst lots of people have come up with lots of ideas, we only just have to acknowledge that the pot is limited, our ability to manage it is limited, so we may have to forego some potentially quite lucrative projects. We've tried to focus in on those [schemes] which actually do fit the strategy.

He also describes the authorisation process:

> It depends on the size of the investment. There are rules which say that, for a small project the decision might be taken by a director of the function but anything over £1.5m would be taken by a multi-discipline team.

An unintended effect of authorisation limits is highlighted by Andy Cook:

> It is amazing, we have £1.5m and the decision goes outside. It is concerning how many projects are for £1.45m. Then we start to sniff.

LUL managers did not express major concerns on financial constraints despite the external perception that LUL is underfunded, except for suggestions that they hoped to see LUL not as 'Moscow Underground' and as a pleasant travelling environment, given appropriate funding. This may well be because managers have, in effect, internalised financial constraints and have therefore muted awareness of them.

The role of the directors

John Vaughan felt that the role of directors was a key issue, and linked this to the role of judgement and also to the *limitations* of financial valuation:

This is where, at the end of the day, the judgement of the directors comes in because the numbers actually fail you. Somebody goes on his guts and that's where they come in.

. . . If you feel that it is not an unreasonable thing to include those things, you actually draw the director's attention to them, that's where they exercise their judgement.

John Vaughan illustrates this further by an example where a director challenged the business case based on that director's personal experience of the tube station. He quotes 'He [the director] used to actually use that station. He didn't believe the numbers that were coming through.'

David Marshall also reflects on this role of the directors, particularly in assessing intangibles and risks:

You can hold the board, or whatever, accountable for that gap because they've made the judgement that that gap is acceptable given the intangibles that have been thrown up.

If there is a project they are there to look at the project evaluation, to see whether the question of risk has been identified, analysed, and at the end of the day to decide whether to tick it.

In both the above cases, therefore, the directors play an important and valuable role in the appraisal process.

Marginal analysis

Another issue concerned with financial tools which surfaces is the use of *marginal analysis*. John Vaughan (LUL) reveals a problem in applying this concept, implying that managers may abuse it:

It seems to me that it is quite legitimate to say we'll only take that part, the marginal cost, into that part of the decision process. I just wonder, sometimes, whether too much use of that route might lead you down all the wrong paths.

David Marshall of Post Office Counters Limited echoes these concerns:

The problem that I have with your space argument is, if you've got space, and you've got two or three projects, you don't take account of that in the evaluation of the project. When you find a fourth project, suddenly you've got a huge investment which at your costs will probably kill them. It's likely to kill that project off because you've got to build a new building, and that concerns me.

Both of the above comments highlight another trap for managers in the use of marginal analysis: they assume that incremental costs are based on short-run costs based on a tactical investment. Yet where the strategy dictates that these 'tactical investments' recur, this may well yield increases in long-run costs. These will be over and above shifts in short-term incremental costs.

Commentary on decision processes:

- A first hurdle to linking strategic and financial appraisal appeared to be that what counts as a 'strategic decision' or project – this was often unclear.
- Uncertainty and ambiguity within the business strategy itself forms a second hurdle to forging closer linkages.
- A third barrier is the fragmentation which occurs because of a multitude of planning and decision-making processes (mission, strategic plans, budgets and project appraisals).
- Formulating clear strategic objectives for projects was a way of making a bridge between strategic and financial appraisal.
- A consequence of implicit or unclear linkages between strategic and financial appraisal appears to be that decision criteria become very ambiguous. Also managers have great difficulty in prioritising investment projects.
- In both companies the directors appear to play an involved role in helping resolve ambiguity.
- Finally, marginal analysis presents difficulties when managers assume that costs which are fixed short-term are also fixed long-term.

CONTROLS

Financial controls and *post implementation controls* surface as an important issue. John Vaughan identifies a gap in existing processes:

> What we don't do is say what were the benefits achieved and where are they to be found now? And we don't usually check it back that way. Unless you find some way of checking back you could always find some way of saying this was based on the assumption that this was based on something else. There must be risks there.

Both Andy Cook and David Marshall see measurement of intangibles as a problem area. Andy Cook begins:

> Most things that you see which are intangible may become more tangible a long way off, after the project's been completed. It's a question of accountability in timescales that are 10 years hence.

But one problem arises – David Marshall expands:

> If a district manager actually said, either, he didn't agree with the benefits, or he didn't feel that putting that project in was going to deliver some of the other benefits, the other intangibles, that would be a big minus when the project eventually went up for authority. And it would be such a big minus that probably it wouldn't go ahead. Unfortunately. I say unfortunately because the kind of projects that we are going for at the moment affect all districts.

The problem of implementing both measurement and control systems is aptly summarised by David Marshall (POCL):

> The problem we've got is explaining to people why you need to do all this work, you know, why you need to do investment appraisal in the first place, why you need to do strategic checks, and where you should cut off your expenditure.

The above offers some clues to the role of control systems. First, control systems do not necessarily measure the capture of all of the value incorporated in planning systems. Second they are not necessarily linked to reward (and recognition systems). Also, they may be hard to change – this is particularly important when considering any change to *planning* systems.

Commentary on controls:

- Both LUL and Post Office Counters' managers identify an important problem in ensuring that intangible benefits included in estimates are actually realised and subsequently measured.
- A further tension highlighted by Post Office Counters Limited is where the economic basis of appraisal differs from budgetary and reward and recognition systems.
- Finally, in applying controls managers may frequently meet a silent resistance from many managers who dislike being tied down.

SUBJECTIVE JUDGEMENT

John Vaughan (LUL) identifies historical precedent as another important variable in the decision-making process which places greater strains on judgement where experience of past, similar precedents is lacking:

> Whenever you're going into new things, all the time the argument is that

you can base it on past experience, you know; 'we've never had a past experience of that', 'we've never had one of those before.'

He also reflects on a graphic story of the Moorgate disaster when belief of directors overrode his views of historical precedent:

> Just a quick anecdote. A proposal came up that maybe we should take out some form of catastrophe insurance. I argued strongly that the premium was going to be astronomical. At the time I agreed that, going back fifty or a hundred years there were no possible cases of doing this sort of thing. The director looked at the case, took out catastrophe insurance.
>
> Two years after, Moorgate, the train crash happened. It paid back just like that. Now, on all the statistics that were available, you wouldn't have taken out all that insurance. At the end of the day, perhaps, the role of directors is to quantify all the numbers and you at the end of the day, have to take a judgement.
>
> I think probably that the greater the element of uncertainty, the more you are going to a different activity with a different competitive style, the less the numbers become important and the more the judgement of the people who you have becomes important.

The related issues of acts of faith and subjective belief are surfaced repeatedly at London Underground. John Vaughan describes this:

> People do believe that the numbers mean something which is why they actually have systems in the first place. And then they get something which doesn't actually make sense but they feel very strong . . . They are in that business and they have got some very strong . . . It's that that makes you go back and look at the numbers more carefully.
>
> That's an article of faith, and article of faith decisions are the least certain, because each one is a new article of faith, it's the least relevant to past experience because it's always different.
>
> It is almost impossible to put a value to it [improving staff accommodation]. You can do it, but the analysis is so iffy that it would be a very tortuous process so you come back to, 'you know it makes sense'.
>
> The bean counter says at the same time, here's all your figures, but it's all terribly grey because there is so much uncertainty. At that point, he says to the director, that's all I can give you but the director has to make the decision in this area.

This is also reflected, but to a lesser degree, by Post Office Counters Limited's managers. David Marshall relates 'acts of faith' to investment in security:

> It is a fairly limited amount that we are spending [on security]. It is going to be one of those acts of faith. It is going to be something that the Board can

take a view on. Should we spend a million pounds or should we spend five million pounds?

Commentary

Commenting briefly on subjective judgement we see that managers of both companies identify different aspects of subjective judgement as being influential in shaping the decision process, especially where decisions involve high levels of intangible value, uncertainty and interdependency.

PRACTICAL LESSONS FROM THE CASE ON LONDON UNDERGROUND AND POST OFFICE COUNTERS LIMITED

Value of investment decisions

1. 'Project appraisal' can (and should) cover non-capital projects.
2. Replacement decisions may invite search for better options than a replace on a 'like-for-like' basis. These may involve redefinition of need, or the capture of opportunities to add proportionately more value through enlarging project scope.
3. Definition of projects can be done by either working down from a higher level 'strategic vision', or by working up from a 'base level'.
4. Flexibility may have a value worth capturing in a project definition which defers or delays financial commitment in part or builds in capability to respond to potential opportunity (but at lowest cost).
5. Safety and security investment decisions might be helped by using 'scenario methods' – for instance if a scenario of 'things going wrong' can be pictured then the crucial points of weakness which permit these events to occur can be segregated. Equally, it may be valuable to build-in flexibility in systems to combat threats (eg by building in provision to move cash centres from an area penetrated by criminals at least cost rather than attempt to construct a 'foolproof' solution).
6. Where there is evidence of a very marked decline in the 'base case' then this may suggest that the business strategy requires review as so much investment is needed simply to maintain current position. It may also highlight that whilst incremental investment may generate 'a positive return' the business overall may yield low *average* return on capital employed – as the business needs to run hard financially just to stay still.

7. Intangibles are often amenable to measurement by working backwards from measurement of the market-based or operational benefits from which these are derived. Thus in many cases intangibles *are* quantifiable, if perhaps not financially.

Uncertainty and interdependency

1. Apparent stability of demand may obscure some underlying vulnerabilities (eg for London Underground to the 1991–92 recession, and for Post Office Counters to pressure on clients – government departments – in the event of possible public sector expenditure cuts).
2. Where external stakeholders are less than clear on the objectives for an organisation (whether public or private sector) this can be viewed perhaps as an opportunity to mould their views and values, rather than necessarily as a threat.
3. It may be helpful for managers to distinguish between 'acceptable' and 'unacceptable' levels of risk in formulating investment proposals. Here a careful balance is required between enabling managers to be innovative and entrepreneurial as opposed to giving *carte blanche* to indulge in pet safety or security projects.

Decision processes

1. Greater rigour and consistency in how managers use the word 'strategic' might well avoid many of the problems and disrepute into which the word can fall. This might avoid its use to label 'favoured' projects (this is, in golfing terms, the equivalent of a 'handicap').
2. It should not be surprising if major decisions *do* change during gestation – indeed this may be healthy providing that the sluggish progress of decision-making does not cause major disadvantages through loss of speed which may be crucial to seize market windows of opportunity.
3. In order to formulate clear links between strategic and financial appraisal, it is imperative that 'the strategy' should be communicated in sufficient detail to key decision-makers and advisers.
4. Business cases may be fruitfully compiled in pictorial form rather than (principally) in financial numbers and with (mainly) operational and technical details. Particular areas for representation may include plotting key assumptions to display degrees of perceived certainty

against degrees of financial impact, or of the make up of an investment programme split by strategic objectives.

5. Operational ability to implement investment projects is a crucial success factor but one which may easily be overlooked as self-evident: where the contents of the strategy are partially communicated to implementors then they cannot, realistically, confirm that plans are achievable.

6. Organisations will invariably exhibit a bias towards projects which they are either most comfortable with (traditionally) or where at a particular moment (fashion-wise) they find attractive. Where this encourages significant imbalance in the investment programme, then a *shift in cultural attitudes* may be required to compensate (eg in deliberately setting out to end up with 'some risky projects').

7. Prioritisation is a multisided process which is hard to reduce purely to a simple, financial dimension. This suggests that priorities may be best looked at by examining a mix of quantitative *and* qualitative factors. For instance, a particular decision may appear financially attractive in its own right but have no plausible synergy with existing operations. The latter synergy might count against it as compared with another project where direct returns are more modest but where it adds value, either by protecting the business or by offering contingent opportunities.

8. It is easy for 'incremental' analysis to be applied myopically, without regard to indirect or contingent costs. Managers need to perform the rather difficult act of *going out to look for missing incremental costs* (present and future) in order to avoid this danger.

Controls

1. Intangibles which are claimed to be 'future' may nevertheless invite specification of 'the conditions under which potential value may arise and how it will be harvested'. Once these conditions are specified, managers can then decide whether to try to make value capture more likely by amending their action plans.

2. Line managers may be resistant to attempts to expand measurement systems over areas of less tangible benefit simply because of resistance to perceived 'over-control'.

Subjective judgement

Subjective judgement may involve not merely evaluation of 'hard to quantify' benefits but also the weighing of risk and uncertainty – depending upon the *values* of the individuals performing these subjective judgements, the results may differ considerably.

CONCLUSIONS

This final section now examines the questions raised in the introduction to the case. Again, there appear to be a number of problems which can be generated by having only an implicit linkage of strategic and financial appraisal, as follows:

- Some areas of investment such as in 'image' may not be appraised as such. This lack of a formal mechanism for appraisal may inhibit investment in areas of less tangible benefit.
- The definition of 'what cut' of project to appraise (the 'unit and level of analysis') is obscured without clear linkages between strategic and financial appraisal.
- Intangible value can be better understood by shifting the emphasis onto outward-looking analysis (again by focusing more on strategic appraisal).
- The issues of protective value and the base case require some strategic input for the financial analysis to be meaningful where the external environment is changing.
- Uncertainties in the external environment are made more cloudy where strategic appraisal is scant. In both organisations, the perceived financial constraints appeared to be – at least – partly due to ambiguities in strategy definition.
- Linkages were further undermined by lack of clarity about what the concept 'strategic' actually covered.
- Decision and planning processes were multiple and this makes it easy for strategic and financial linkages to fragment unless processes are kept as simple as possible and consistent effort is made to relate these.
- The involvement of the directors and incorporation of subjective judgement ameliorated some of these problems but is by itself unlikely to be sufficient to forge closer linkages between strategic and financial appraisal.
- Finally, control, reward and recognition systems need to be aligned with economic bases of appraisal: this is one of the most difficult tasks of all.

To conclude, the London Underground and Post Office Counters Limited cases highlight the following factors:

- When the decision process appears to be getting more difficult and complex, managers can be easily drawn into working ever harder to produce 'accurate' financial appraisals.
- As the 'strategy' is often taken as a separate matter from project appraisal and as a 'given', managers may also not be aware that many of their problems can be traced back to the incomplete linkage between strategic and financial appraisal.
- Once managers *do* realise, in the analytical sense, that this is one of the key causes of their problems, this presents an even bigger problem, that of managing the change required to modify decision processes so as to forge these linkages throughout this process.

The case in Chapter 8 on BP now takes us forward into that change process in a major company which has worked over several years to bridge strategic and financial appraisal.

8

CASE ON SHAREHOLDER VALUE – BP

INTRODUCTION

This chapter follows the argument already spelt out – that strategy and value are complementary perspectives on business management. We have already seen in preceding chapters that many of the problems associated with making corporate investment decisions are attributable to an unnecessary schizophrenia between strategic and financial appraisal. In this chapter we explore how 'value-based management' has contributed to making corporate investment decisions to maximise shareholder value within BP Group.

Data for this study came from a variety of sources over the period 1989 to 1991. A research workshop was run as a pilot for a dozen managers involved in planning within BP; BP and Rolls Royce corporate planners held a cross-organisational meeting to explore the idea of 'shareholder value'; there was a visit to the consultants who facilitated early stages of implementation of value-based management (or VBM), and finally an interview took place with the project leader responsible for introducing change within planning and control systems during the late 1980s through to 1990.

This account of 'value-based management' at BP is explored as follows:

- Background to value-based management at BP
- Evolution of the process
- Reflections on the BP experience.

BACKGROUND TO VALUE-BASED MANAGEMENT AT BP

Although no one will need reminding that BP is an oil company, by the

159

early 1980s BP Group had diversified into a number of areas including chemicals, coal, gas, minerals and nutritions. This diversification strategy led to increasing difficulty in allocating investment resource between the various divisions of BP. A large central corporate planning department assisted BP's senior executives to make corporate investment decisions from head office but this advisory task was progressively transferred to the international business in line with a policy towards decentralisation.

In common with many other large groups, BP's corporate strategy then experienced a major shift in the mid-1980s. Sir Peter Walters, then Chairman, began a programme of refocusing BP's corporate portfolio in order to concentrate on BP Group's core competences which were in oil and closely related businesses. In a series of disposals and acquisitions, BP rebalanced its portfolio of businesses to once again concentrate primarily on the oil business but retaining businesses with clear and tangible synergies – principally chemicals. This rebalancing included the disposal of mineral activities to RTZ, the acquisition of Britoil and also of the remaining 50 per cent stake in the Sohio associate company. BP's nutritions division was all that remained as an indirectly related business – but the strategic logic here was the very strong competitive position which BP had built up by a sequence of well-managed acquisitions.

Arguably, therefore, the task of making corporate investment decisions in BP should have been made much simpler by these developments at corporate level. But problems of mixing corporate investment decisions within a strategic *and* financial framework remained. The process of simplifying the 'businesses BP is in' had highlighted some important residual problems. These were concerned with linking these decisions with BP's corporate planning process, its control process and ultimately with its rewards systems.

EVOLUTION OF THE PROCESS

The evolution of Value-Based Management (VBM) at BP can be split into four separate phases:

1. Diagnosis – the 'Performance Measurement Review'
2. Piloting VBM
3. Implementation – VBM planning processes
4. Implementation – VBM control and rewards systems.

Diagnosis

The diagnosis phase began in 1986 when top management at BP initiated a major review entitled a 'performance measurement review'. This grew out of concerns about the relevance of 'Return on Capital Employed' (ROCE) as a measure of corporate and business performance.

BP's managers felt uncomfortable with ROCE for several main reasons:

- ROCE is based on financial accounting measures. These measures do not necessarily reflect how successful the business is in generating shareholder value.
- ROCE is backward- rather than forward-looking: it measures past and recent performance rather than the business' capability of generating future cash flows.
- Whilst BP's managers were asked to make decisions on the basis of future cash flows, paradoxically they were judged and rewarded on the basis of performance measures which are accounting-based and historic.

When the 'Performance Measurement Review' team first reported back the practical problems caused by using ROCE, they also identified an approach called 'value management' which the team felt 'might be worth taking a look at'.

Coincidentally, about the same time in the US the idea of 'shareholder value management' was beginning to take firm root. Although the genesis of the 'value movement' began perhaps as early as the very late 1970s in the US, it was given an evolutionary 'push' by the work of Alfred Rappaport. As explained in Chapter 4, Rappaport synthesised ideas from Michael Porter's framework on competitive strategy with the concept that a business strategy could be evaluated as a stream of cash flows, just as if it were a 'capital project'.

Rappaport's framework thus combined corporate finance theory with the notion that shareholder value could be assessed by examining the discounted cash flows of business strategies. The final and crucial ingredient in this framework, however, was the concept of *testing* the financial assumptions underlying cash flows of a business against realistic and robust assumptions on the competitive environment and competitive position. Rappaport suggested that the main 'drivers of value' which generated NPV were directly related to the business' external environment and competitive position. Rappaport believed that it was through deeper understanding of how these drivers impacted on the future cash flows of the business that improved strategic decisions could be made.

Coming back to the case of BP, top management felt that this idea of 'value' offered further promise. Even though there was relatively little precedent for this approach in the UK, it was felt that the matter was worth exploring further. BP began the next phase of the study by working together with a US firm of consultants with experience of 'value-based management' to explore its potential for BP.

The consultants were given the following brief. First, to have a 'quick look' at what BP's corporate portfolio might be worth in terms of NPV of the projected results of existing business strategies. Second, to take a more 'in-depth' look at some *specific* areas of BP where value was being created or lost.

Piloting VBM

The second pilot phase of this exercise was an eye-opener for both BP management and the consultants, even though both parties were sophisticated in their use of strategic and financial planning techniques.

A number of the early insights for BP were:

- Some (though not all) of BP's newer activities created less value than had previously been believed. For example, in one case it was revealed that BP's competitive advantage in a market not closely related to its core businesses was lacking.
- Through examining BP's value chain under a microscope, it was found that whereas in most cases the picture of where shareholder value was created matched previous BP thinking, in a number of notable areas it did not. This raised some key strategic questions about some business areas. These not only concerned their competitive position and market attractiveness but also whether they represented value-creating opportunities sufficiently large to be worth pursuing.

The consultants were also exposed to a learning process as they grappled with the specific problems posed by BP's strategy, structure and finances. Particularly contentious was that of BP's corporate cost of capital. Although both BP and the consultants agreed on the appropriate rate to use there was some technical debate as to how to arrive at that rate. This may seem, at first sight, to be an academic issue as both sides agreed on the actual rate to use. However, this was not simply academic as potential changes in BP's mix of businesses, financial structure and perception by the stock market might well result subsequently in the two approaches giving significantly different answers.

Some of the key lessons from this second phase of development of VBM were:

- VBM is not a 'magic tool' or black box which will answer all planning and control difficulties at a stroke – it needs to be applied and tailored intelligently to its specific context.

- Applying VBM is an ongoing learning process – not only about how value is generated or lost in the business but also about how to use the tools themselves.
- Any company thinking of applying VBM should avoid overselling the process. Expectations also need to be carefully managed, particularly concerning the lead time to implementation.

The pilot phase thus established VBM as being the core framework for corporate planning and corporate investment decision-making in BP Group. The 'pilot' enabled the infrastructure to be set in place for the roll-out into planning processes throughout the BP Group.

VBM planning processes

During the third phase of development of VBM, the process was successively and successfully applied in BP's international businesses. This roll-out was coordinated by BP's internal team, who worked hand in hand with BP's business managers in their ongoing planning and decision-making processes.

According to the (then) project leader of the team, Simon Woolley:

Where you applied VBM, there were always surprises. For example, I was sitting with one BP manager and we were looking at a model of his business which represented his future profitability and cash flows from operations and key assumptions about the market. The manager explained that it was easy to generate additional value through business growth as profitability was increased.

But we then played a 'what-if' scenario which increased the growth rate of part of the business using a cash flow model of the business' operations. The manager was shocked when the NPV of the business strategy *actually went down*. This was because the 'growth' was not 'profitable growth' in value-based terms: although it was apparently profitable on an accounting basis, once an allowance for the time value of money had been made and particularly adjustment for additional working capital, it was not. This taught us a lot about the business as it not only raised questions about incremental value creation but also about the quality of opportunity facing this business and its competitive position.

Simon Woolley then goes on to describe how managers found the use of VBM during this key phase:

At first managers appeared to expect absolute answers to an imprecise problem – measuring value creation. As they learnt more about VBM they began to realise that the value of VBM lies not so much in absolute measurement but in its power of making comparisons.

For example, VBM really comes into its own when comparing major strategic decisions or options for a particular decision. It is also useful for comparing different *financing* options – which I would stress again is a *separate issue* to evaluating the strategic opportunity itself.

Obviously it also enables you to post-audit your decision after the event. Finally it enables you to benchmark your performance relative to your competition.

If I might expand on the latter point, we are now at the point where we don't simply say, 'what a great performance last quarter' – just because the oil price has leapt up. We compare our performance not just against what we said we expected to achieve but also against how specific competitors have done in the same or similar environment.

The strong impression gained from this account is that implementation of VBM is something which does not happen overnight but is a gradual process involving sustained learning and continual effort. Recognising the need to share this learning, Simon Woolley set up a 'corporate network' for debating VBM within BP Group. This network is a meeting of practitioners of VBM across BP businesses which meet off-site to debate and agree 'best practice' VBM methods and to spread the 'VBM message'.

VBM control and rewards systems

Phase 4, which was implementing VBM control and rewards systems occurred during 1990–91. Only recently have the first full year's plans under VBM been monitored and controlled. Again, this has provoked healthy debate concerning what factors might have been 'controllable' versus those which were 'uncontrollable'. VBM therefore involves not merely *measurement* but also the ability to interpret these measures against a background of change. Because of this, VBM should not be applied through exact and rigid controls, but should be sensitive to external context and also tolerant of areas of unavoidable measurement error.

By the stage of implementation, VBM needed to become *the* language of planning control and rewards systems. The latter issue is of considerable interest as management behaviour is unlikely to change materially.

At BP a parallel review of corporate rewards systems was begun in the late-1980s which proved to be an opportune moment to align these systems to VBM. In order to achieve this linkage, Human Resources specialists were introduced to the rationale of VBM. This involved a switch away from ROCE-based measures to VBM-based performance measures.

The application of VBM-based rewards systems does, however, raise further issues which needed to be addressed at BP. Although a lot of work has been done to link top managers' rewards to shareholder value at BP Group level which was benchmarked externally, difficulties remained at senior and middle levels of management. Recent work has been done on linking these rewards to value generation at the business level. For functional heads it has been found possible to target and measure performance against specific value and cost drivers. A framework of 'critical success factors' is then established for optimising value and cost drivers so that managers can be targeted on achievement against these factors. This recognises that managers should be rewarded for how they succeed in controlling these levers which drive value in the business. Thus the focus is away from being purely an historic performance which mixes controllable versus uncontrollable factors together.

This phase of the change process was perhaps the most difficult of all as it most directly affected managers individually. As VBM is not an exact 'scientific tool' rewards systems need to be set up which capture broad measures of performance rather than exact levels of achievement.

REFLECTIONS ON THE BP EXPERIENCE

BP's experience of VBM over the past five years raises a number of broader lessons about linking strategic and financial appraisal, about the role this can play in the management process, and in how change of this kind can be implemented.

First, BP's experience reveals that VBM can bring together a variety of key elements in the management process, including:

- strategic and financial planning at corporate and business levels;
- corporate investment decisions, including organic investment, acquisitions and divestments;
- evaluating revenue expenditure programmes;
- in corporate finance, dividend policy, investor relations, treasury management, financing decisions and tax planning;
- performance targeting and measurement and rewards systems.

The following summarises critical success factors which might enable implementation of VBM:

- Top management being visibly committed to, and are actively interested in, VBM.

- 'Value' to shareholders being set alongside ambitions to satisfy other corporate values. It should not be seen as the *sole* objective of the organisation (unless that is what the 'corporate mission' says).
- `VBM needs to embrace planning, control *and* rewards systems.
- Managers are being trained already to use cash-based financial tools (DCF) *and* have been exposed to strategic analysis tools.
- Willingness exists to explore areas where value may not be currently optimised.
- Early handover of management of the process to management – rather than championed by external consultants.
- Having a clear plan early on for a roll-out programme throughout the organisation.
- Managing expectations so that managers will realise that the lags will occur between investing in change and reaping the rewards.

On the other hand there are a number of areas to avoid in implementation of VBM. First, there is a danger that VBM could degenerate into a 'number crunching' exercise where financial modelling takes on a life of its own. Second, one can fall into the trap of playing the 'VBM-game' through manipulating terminal values of business strategies – these need to be as tested against external assumptions rather than added on simply as a notional multiple of earnings. Third, VBM should not be applied only to a particular area of the management process or business – for example, purely to capital investment decisions or to core decisions but not to newer business areas. Finally, it is sometimes tempting to accept compromise in order to make headway – for example deciding to defer indefinitely any changes in rewards systems during the roll-out programme.

CONCLUSION

To conclude the BP case, it may be useful to summarise some of the key benefits which have come out of the migration to VBM over a five-year transition period:

- BP now has a common framework for integrating long-range strategic plans, capital programmes, acquisitions and divestment business cases and short-term budgets.
- This is also being married to its rewards systems so that behaviour and motivation are aligned to decision and control processes.
- In specific areas of its operations, BP has decided either to divest or refocus its businesses.

- VBM is also being applied increasingly to test value generated by major elements of cost in its revenue budgets.
- There has also been a realisation that a trade-off not only exists between large investment projects but also between value generated by these and by revenue cost programmes.
- Some notable 'prizes' have been won through using VBM to make financing decisions, with direct and measurable impact on shareholder value at corporate level.
- Finally, performance management at BP has become much more outward-focused and geared to achievements relative to competitors and also relative to market conditions.

This case needs to be set alongside the previous chapters, where we explored how managers faced a raft of major difficulties in linking strategic and financial appraisal. Although the difficulties faced by BP in implementing VBM were no doubt equally large, the case emphasises the need to avoid 'piecemeal' efforts to bridge strategic and financial appraisal. But it also underlines the potential benefits from grasping the nettle of change in strategic and financial thinking.

Readers who are practising managers may now be wondering how they might set about putting into practice the ideas from BP and the other four cases. The first steps for change might involve applying value management techniques in unison with strategic analysis for a discrete business area or decision as a *pilot.* This should give a beach-head for changing planning and control systems. But, as highlighted by the BP case, efforts to roll-out change in planning and control processes which are fragmented will be frustrated unless existing approaches are dismantled. Also, unless management is prepared to adapt their *appraisal style,* then early successes may end in little real progress.

Implementing value management is very much a learning process (which will be greatly helped by the analysis tools in Appendix 1). But the really difficult barrier to change is modifying the management process itself: this can be akin to persuading a driver of a car to change his steering wheel – whilst he is driving – for a better one. Expert guidance may be needed to ensure he stays on the road.

PART THREE – IMPLICATIONS

IMPLICATIONS FOR BRIDGING STRATEGIC AND FINANCIAL VALUE

INTRODUCTION

Chapter 9 draws together the implications for bridging strategic and financial appraisal from the four cases on IDV, Rolls Royce, London Underground and Post Office Counters. This is set out as follows:

- Comparison of context and tools
- Comparison of problems
- Revisiting 'the linkage problem'
- Overall conclusions

This chapter therefore enables the reader to gain a complete overview of the problems managers face and also how they might set about dealing with them. The scope of the chapter is large and it is therefore advised that the reader prepares for this by setting aside a clear hour to reflect fully on the implications for his/her business.

COMPARISON OF CONTEXT AND TOOLS

This section briefly describes the contexts of the four cases on Rolls Royce, IDV, London Underground and Post Office Counters Limited in order to set the scene for our overall findings and recommendations for management practice.

Rolls Royce Aeroengines

First, Rolls Royce Aeroengines' main investment thrust is expenditure on new product development and launch. Although this is a tangible area of spend, the benefits of this investment are very difficult to predict and there appears to be a high degree of uncertainty derived principally from external factors. This uncertainty is compounded by the very long time horizons underpinning these investments.

Rolls Royce managers approach the problem of evaluation of opportunity using a variety of financial tools including DCF but the decision process does not seem to be primarily 'financially-led'. Other, softer factors are employed to judge the logic of appraisal but these do not seem to be heavily structured by use of *strategic* tools.

IDV

The IDV case highlights a very different context. With the exception of acquisitions and long-term brand investment, most areas of spend appear to be shorter-term than Rolls Royce. But the longer-term business environment is becoming increasingly uncertain due to changes in European markets, thus sharing parallel features with Rolls Royce.

IDV's appraisal problems appear to revolve around brands which are difficult to appraise. Acquisitions, though being impacted on by external change, are also evaluated primarily using financial tools. This emphasis on detailed financial appraisal, particularly of capital spend and on acquisitions, helps conserve resources and may lead indirectly to strategic questioning of investment projects and the conservation of investment resource generally. Since the research study, IDV managers have invested increasing effort in external analysis.

London Underground

Next, London Underground invests in a variety of tangible and less tangible areas of investment. Following recent changes over the last few years, the balance of spend has moved more towards greater investment in safety and other less tangible areas such as image. London Underground's *competitive* environment is not seen by managers as being highly uncertain. However, this is compensated for by the perceived impact of political and governmental influences which is part driven by pressure from customer expectations.

London Underground's managers employ a variety of methods with financial criteria being balanced by operational and market analysis. A major issue is the sheer number of investment projects which require appraisal and the difficulty of prioritising these. The projects are appraised traditionally on an incremental basis but are seen increasingly as forming groups or 'investment thrusts'.

Post Office Counters Limited

Post Office Counters invests in a number of different thrusts in its network and supporting infrastructure. Many of the benefits from this investment are less tangible and difficult to measure. Although in the shorter-term the business market is not so volatile as in the private sector cases, in the longer-term there are threats of decline and loss of custom.

The main tools which were in evidence in Post Office Counters were financial ones, but these were supplemented with some operational and market analysis tools. Managers perceive tight financial constraints existing, which aggravates the problems of prioritising investment projects. In addition, the competitive style and scope of the business is seen as constrained because Post Office Counters is a public body. These twin constraints made it harder to invest in newer areas of business to generate growth or to renew existing products and services through quantum shifts in technology base.

Since the research study many of the weaker linkages between strategic and financial appraisal have been tightened by POCL managers.

Summary of common issues

The common issues in linking strategic and financial appraisal are therefore as follows:

- These four organisations employ (to varying degrees) planning processes in which external analysis plays a typically less predominant role than internally or operationally-led analysis. However in each instance, steps were or are now being taken to move towards remedying this apparent imbalance.
- All these organisations operate in external environments which appear 'uncertain', but again in varying degrees, from acute to mild.
- The degree to which external and internal environments can be foreseen with reasonable accuracy throughout the lifetime of business investment projects varied considerably. In some cases the 'zone of foreseeability' ended significantly before the lifetime of investment cash flows.
- Financial criteria were used with differing degrees of sophistication. Although these were seen as important in evaluating the outputs from the decision-making process, their utility appeared to crumble when dealing with softer areas of 'value' which were either inherently hard to define (with precision) or which were of a future and contingent nature.

COMPARISON OF PROBLEMS

This section highlights the main similarities and differences between problems faced by managers in the four cases. This is dealt with as follows:

- Key similarities across all four cases
- Key differences between cases
- Summary of analysis problems
- Summary of process problems
- Key lessons.

Key similarities across all four case histories

Despite differences in the businesses of the four companies, many issues are *generic* across these cases, in particular:

- Managers still tended to regard investment decisions, with the exception of acquisitions, as being mainly those of a 'capital' nature. Yet in all cases managers appeared to have most trouble with those that were either inherently less tangible (for example image or brands) or where the benefits of the investment were part tangible in nature.
- The concept of what the business 'strategy' is *was not always clear*. Also, the definition of what was a 'strategic decision' or what might count as 'strategic *investment* decisions' was one which provoked considerable debate and was far from self-evident. Although it is not a radically new idea to highlight that managers are often less than clear on 'strategy', this is obviously an important barrier to linking strategy and financial appraisal. For instance, it is not even obvious what investment decisions to apply strategic appraisal to, unless managers are clear on what projects are 'strategic'.
- Major barriers to building linkages between strategic and financial appraisal emerged as being:

  a) the ambiguity of the definition of 'the strategy' itself;
  b) the partial communication of the strategy to key advisers involved in (strategic) decision making; and
  c) a lack of explicit strategic objectives for individual projects.

- In all four cases, managers also had major problems in dealing with uncertainty, risk and interdependency. These tended to cloud the financial analysis. Many of these problems might be alleviated through analysis of underlying forces driving value using strategic appraisal tools. For example, the issue of valuing intangible benefits through improved customer service might be addressed by assessment of which customers benefited, how value was being added and also to what extent this value could be captured in the form of higher price, higher volumes, lower discounts or lower risks of switching and loss of business.

- Managers sometimes experienced difficulties in deciding which financial tools to use and when, particularly the use of payback versus IRR versus NPV.
- *Controls* were also revealed to be a very important influence in all cases. The influence of control routines and financial measures generally appears to 'drive backwards' to influence how managers handle earlier stages of the decision process. This may inhibit appraisal of 'softer areas' of value and the inclusion of less tangible value within business cases.
- Finally, subjective judgement emerged as being an important influence in the decision process. This judgement was used to counterbalance cases of incomplete (financial) valuation of opportunity, to help absorb uncertainty and to minimise the fear which is generated by uncertainty. It could also serve as a means through which senior management could intervene on the appraisal without 'upsetting the apple cart' of more detailed appraisal work.

Key differences between cases

Although there were also some key differences between cases it was surprising that these appear relatively few in number given the variety of business and organisational contexts involved. These differences can be quickly summarised by comparing two pairs of cases, first Rolls Royce and IDV and second, London Underground and Post Office Counters.

Rolls Royce and IDV

Key differences include divergences on the extent to which the *value* of contingent elements of opportunities involves purely a comparison of quantified value or whether it involves comparison of quantified value *plus* non-quantified value. In IDV in practice, managers compared only quantified value whereas in Rolls Royce managers appeared to balance not only quantified but also unquantified value. As a separate issue, timescales for recouping investment are much longer for Rolls Royce generally than for IDV. Finally, there are major differences in the degree to which a declining *base case* is considered to be acceptable. The factors highlighted sharp differences in appraisal style between both companies as a result of variations in well-embedded planning and control routines.

London Underground and Post Office Counters

The main difference between these is that London Underground managers appear to incorporate a relatively higher proportion of *value* (including less tangible value) within their business cases than Post Office Counters' managers. With the above exception both organisations showed significant similarities in processes and style.

Summary of analysis problems

The key underlying problem themes which emerged from the four cases (and which are likely to be shared similarly by many other organisations) include the degree of competitive uncertainty, the degree of uncertainty of internal policy and objectives or 'clarity of strategic vision', the timescales for recouping investment outlays, and finally the valuation style used. In the latter case this may involve whether and how less tangible factors are included.

Table 9.1 contains an overview of these four factors across the four cases.

Rolls Royce faces an acute problem of timescales for recouping investment reaching well beyond foreseeable market conditions and more specifically the competitive prospects for each product launch. This is compounded by external interdependencies which Rolls Royce managers appear to find difficulty in including within the formal comparison of opportunities.

IDV also faces a high degree of future competitive uncertainty but managers have clear internal financial objectives to guide appraisal. Also, much of their (non-brand) investment programme (especially 'capital') has relatively shorter-term horizons. IDV's financial appraisal tools and controls appear to fit the needs of that part of their investment programme with short-term time horizons.

However, brand investment and also acquisitive investments have much longer time horizons and benefits are inherently harder to quantify. The difficulty of formulating specific strategic objectives for brands combined with IDV's preference to exclude less tangible benefits from formal appraisals makes this a harder area to address.

Table 9.1 Comparison of key strategic and financial themes between cases – analytical issues

Problem theme	Rolls Royce	IDV	London Underground	Post Office Counters
Degree of perceived competitive uncertainty	Very high	High	Low	Low but could become high
Degree of perceived uncertainty of strategic and financial objectives 'strategic vision'	Financial objectives part certain	Financial objectives certain, strategic less certain	Strategic objectives uncertain, financial fairly certain*	Strategic & financial objectives uncertain (as at 1989)*
Timescales for recouping outlays	Cash inflows (including spares) for up to 30 years	Variable – from 1 year to ongoing (for brands)	Cash inflows for up to 30 years	Variable – from 1 year to up to 10 years)
Valuation style – intangibles and inter-dependencies	Less tangibles incorporated in overall judgement but not quantified	Exclude less tangible benefits altogether	Formally include in the value	Partly include in the value

* Note: Both London Underground Limited and Post Office Counters Limited have (since 1989) reached a much clearer picture of their strategic and financial objectives

London Underground has very long timescales for investment but this appears mitigated by an apparently more stable, competitive environment than that experienced by Rolls Royce or IDV. However, uncertainty of strategic objectives makes it harder to manage the decision process and linkages between strategic and financial appraisal. Managers are more relaxed in evaluating less tangible areas financially as this was consistent with managers' planning routines and style.

Post Office Counters faces a potentially uncertain external environment, yet its timescales for commitment of investment for some projects may extend beyond the zone of 'ready foreseeability'. Also, the degree of uncertainty over internal strategic and financial objectives (or 'clarity of strategic vision') appears to further cloud the appraisal. These factors combine to aggravate already difficult problems of evaluating a base case for the overall business. Without investment this may be in decline. The base case may also be clouded by interdependencies between investment thrusts including image building, automation, property investment and refurbishment.

Finally, both Post Office Counters and London Underground managers formally incorporate a value for less tangible benefits within investment cases. This provides a potentially closer linkage between strategic and financial appraisal, but in the very act of doing this problems of control and measurement post implementation are generated.

Summary of process problems

The main process issues which surfaced were:

- Planning and control routines: these were apparently influential (but in differing ways) in all four cases. Managers differed in how rigorously and rigidly they pursued planning measures through implementation and into post-review.
- Reliance on explicit sharing of 'subjective judgement': this proved both useful and necessary where analysis was clouded by intangible and contingent value, where there was a lack of historic precedent or where 'the numbers' indicated a picture contrary to that felt by individual managers or directors.
- Financial criteria: there were some clear differences in managers' preferences for particular tools, key influences being duration of project, the degree of implicit 'favour' by top management (with shorter payback being used to test less favoured projects in one company), and finally personal comfort levels in using a particular financial tool. IRR appeared to command centre-stage overall in managers' thinking but was often used in parallel with NPV.

The issues above are combined with those identified as more of an 'analytical' nature to distil a framework of grasping the entire linkage problem shown in Figure 9.1.

Key lessons

The above in depth comparison of the four core cases enables us to break down the problem of linking strategic and financial appraisal of major investment decisions into two elements, the first of which is demand-related and the second is supply-related.

Demand-related problems

In dealing with demand-related problems, some areas of investment are inherently hard to evaluate (strategically and financially) in view of the compounding effects of increased uncertainty over time and of interdependency effects. This may provoke a natural reaction of *fear* which managers may understandably seek to repress. The idea of intangibles appears to be a blanket category to cover cash flows which are uncertain or beneficial effects which are inherently hard to measure (either due to interdependency or simply because measurement *precision* is not available). Intangibles may also involve subtle interdependencies such as the synergistic value of sets of investment projects, interrelationships of investment programmes with operational change, and also value destroying influences such as loss of competitive focus, and finally the substitution of one cash generating activity for another.

Supply-related problems

In dealing with supply-related problems, managers do not find it easy to cope with the degree of ambiguity which these involve. This might be achieved, for example, through insightful and holistic thinking, through the use of strategic, financial and other tools and also through being able to blend these appropriately within the management process. A further ingredient appears to be the harnessing of *subjective judgement* within the appraisal process. This may play an important role not merely as a substitute for analysis or as an 'uncertainty absorber', but as a way of cementing otherwise isolated or fragmented views of an opportunity at crucial stages of the decision process.

Implementation and control-related problems

In dealing with these problems, the 'appraisal' process cannot be unhooked from the implications of follow-through to implementation. Where 'value' is assumed to exist (especially 'soft' value), managers appear to feel uncomfortable without orderly flow through to measurement control, and indeed without links to reward (or punishment). The power of these latter control (and reward) stages 'drives backwards' to influence decision-making. This feature is a central issue for managers contemplating change in appraisal systems.

This suggests that no 'right' or 'best mix' of analytical tools and appraisal process exists across all businesses regardless of internal or external context. However, it does suggest that the tools should be closely matched to the appraisal task and context in any particular environment.

As a final output to this chapter comparing cases, Figure 9.1 displays six key elements which emerged as being at the core of the appraisal problem.

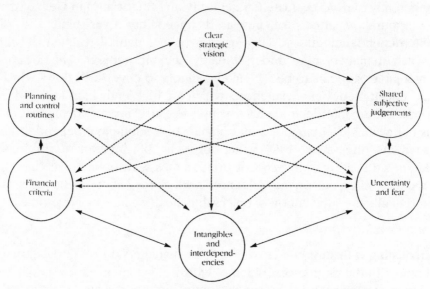

Figure 9.1 Overview of six key issues in linking strategic and financial appraisal

A selection of the key questions which the framework in Figure 9.1 suggests for the practitioner are:

- To what extent is there a clear strategic vision underlying the view of the base case and the with-investment case, and does this provide adequate support for the financial projections?
- Are subjective judgements surfaced and tested systematically in order to challenge and refine both quantitative and qualitative assumptions?
- Are key uncertainties fully explored or is this repressed by key individuals or within the appraisal team as a whole due to underlying fear?
- Is a consistent and 'fair' approach taken to evaluate intangibles and interdependencies, and are control measures set for them?
- Are financial criteria applied in a haphazard fashion and are the numbers used proactively as a stimulus for generating strategic questions?

- Do decision routines severely constrain 'thinking about the whole' of the problem or opportunity, by focusing purely on narrowly-defined, incremental analysis, and without linkage to data and judgements in other planning processes?
- Are all six elements in Figure 9.1 working harmoniously together as a managed whole, or are one or more elements in conflict with others?

The second part of this chapter moves on to address how greater cohesion and vision can be achieved in practice, taking each problem area in turn. This draws from the Cranfield empirical research and makes some practical suggestions for implementing change.

REVISITING THE LINKAGE PROBLEM

This part of the chapter revisits the linkage problem, dealing with the following areas:

- Overview of the linkages
- Process and macro-level
- Analytical and content linkages and tensions
- Decision process and organisational learning
- Summary and conclusions.

OVERVIEW OF THE LINKAGES

The issue of 'linking strategic and financial appraisal' appears to be not a single problem, but a family of problems. From past theory, we might mentally picture a wide river that we are attempting to bridge from two predetermined points. But managers' perspectives reveal that there are no two single ends of the 'strategy-finance' bridge, and therefore it is hardly surprising that managers struggle to make 'one-to-one' and simple linkages between a single thing called 'finance' and a single thing called 'strategy'. Figure 9.2 highlights this graphically by distinguishing between linkages at the process, analytical and at the decision levels, and also between areas of tension.

Process linkages include macro-level connections such as mission and the impact of internal and external change on both investment mix and resource allocation. Analytical linkages include the possible valuation of a strategy or substrategy and also going beyond 'financial value' to its underlying competitive determinants. Decision linkages include a raft of more-difficult-to-quantify areas of value, including uncertainty, inter-dependency, intangibles, protective and contingent value.

Finally, tensions include the clash between economic and accounting-based measures of performance, the realities of financial constraint and use of financial tools as targeting vehicles. It also includes behavioural factors such as the credibility-building process within decision-making and also the impact of control measures which influence the scope of areas of value which managers feel comfortable about including in the business case.

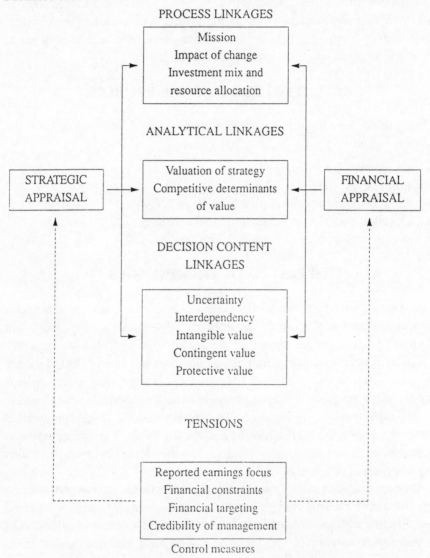

Figure 9.2 Complex linkages and tensions between strategic and financial appraisal

The 'linkages' above thus appear to be a network of issues. The problem of 'making the linkage' between strategic and financial appraisal is further compounded by the diversity of types and contexts of investment decision (see the four cases summarised in the earlier part of this chapter).

PROCESS AND MACRO-LEVEL

This section suggests that managers may find it very difficult to link strategic and financial appraisal without exploring certain macro-level linkages in greater depth. A number of key issues emerged in Chapters 6 and 7 which can now be best unravelled by differentiating between 'macro-level' and 'micro-level' content linkages. 'Macro-level' covers linkages between major influences or systems in the management process. 'Micro-level' covers linkage problems at the core of making a specific investment decision and which are therefore of a more detailed, analytical nature.

At the macro-level, the main, potential linkages appear to be *a)* between elements of corporate mission, strategy and value, and *b)* between strategy, change and investment mix.

Figure 9.3 describes some key potential linkages between corporate mission, strategy and value (in each case the direction of the arrow shows the path of influence). First, *mission* emerged as an important element which may enable managers to think more holistically about investment decisions. Although mission may seem remote from investment decision-making at first sight, it may provide a guide for *what* to be investing in, and equally the financial signals arising from investment appraisal may be indicators of whether a mission is appropriate (ie does it add value?). 'Mission' was a term used by managers themselves at London Underground, the Post Office and at Rolls Royce Aeroengines – therefore we have to understand it from their perspective, rather than being preoccupied with academic preconceptions. At London Underground, the business mission was related to goals like making the underground a safe and pleasant place to travel through. At Post Office Counters this mission also appeared to relate to customer focus. At Rolls Royce the word 'mission' was used because managers preferred the idea of 'strategic intent' as an overarching guide to strategic thinking.

The main *potential* linkages between corporate mission, strategy and value were as follows:

- Between corporate mission and the strategy: potential linkages include first, to check the achievability of the mission – at London Underground, for example, the new mission suggested the need for a strategy – subsequently captured in the 1991 'company plan'. Second, the mission could be used to provide a framework of strategic objectives for use in investment appraisal (as at both London Underground and at Post Office Counters).

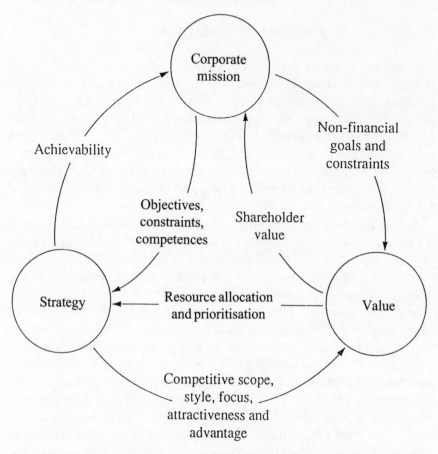

Figure 9.3 Possible linkages of corporate mission, strategy and value

- Between corporate mission and value: potential linkages include introducing into the mission the idea of value-seeking and creating activity (related to shareholder value). Also the idea of non-financial goals and constraints may be used to guide 'permissible' value creating opportunity, thus giving the idea of 'strategic fit' more bite (as in the BP case in Chapter 8).
- Between strategy and value: first, potential linkages include the ideas of competitive scope, style, focus, attractiveness and competitive

advantage. Second, financial appraisal may be used to procure resource from both internal and external sources, and of course to prioritise investment projects. These issues are taken up in more detail in the next section on micro-linkages.

In all four core cases (Chapters 6 and 7) some, but not all, of these linkages had been cemented – this incomplete linkage no doubt contributed to managers' appraisal difficulties.

The second macro-linkage was that of linking strategy, change and the investment mix (Figure 9.4.)

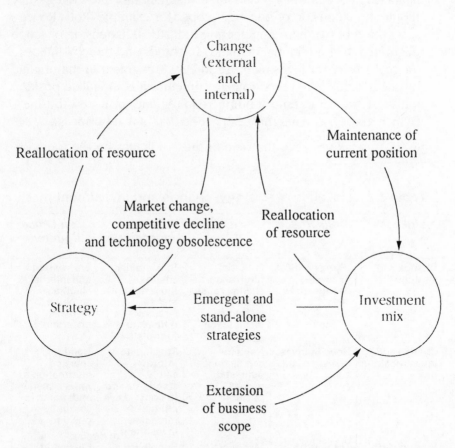

Figure 9.4 Possible linkages of strategy, change and investment mix

Figure 9.4 indicates some key linkages as follows:

- Linkages between change and strategy: from the four cases, external market change, competitive decline and technology obsolescence are among the many factors which feed into the need to adjust the strategy. Equally, the strategy may also lead to reallocation of resource (for example, following the Kings Cross Disaster LUL refocused its resources onto safety).

- Linkages between change and investment mix: the rate of external and internal change may increase the need for investment simply to maintain current competitive position and scope. Also, the planned investment mix may be used to reallocate resources therefore involving (internal) change.
- Linkages between strategy and the investment mix: the strategy may require an extension of business scope (for example, Rolls Royce's acquisition of Northern Engineering Industries). Extension of scope might generate additional demands for funds and thereby intensify internal rivalry for investment resources. Investment in the original business scope is required to maintain current competitive position whilst at the same time funding requirements of a new business (which may exceed internal cash generation of that business).

Table 9.2 now summarises the state of these linkages for the four core cases.

Table 9.2 Linkages of strategy, change and investment mix

Linkages	Rolls Royce	IDV	London Underground	Post Office Counters
Change and strategy	High degree of external change makes strategy formulation difficult	Potential future external change causes problems in strategy formulation	Stakeholder change (government) makes strategy difficult to formulate	Both external and internal change combine to increase uncertainty
Change and investment mix	Need to invest in R&D to 'stay still'	Need for acquisitions to build and protect position	Pressure to improve safety standards and to boost LUL's image refocuses investment	Need for selected automation to reduce costs and maintain competitive position
Strategy and investment mix	Traditional focus has been organic but a recent, large acquisition complicates picture	Mix of organic and acquisitive 'hard' and 'soft' areas of investment – prioritisation made difficult	Prioritisation difficult due partly to the strategy being less than clear (as at 1990)	Clear shift towards investing in projects within core strategies

Table 9.2 helps illuminate the earlier cases as follows:

- For Rolls Royce (as at 1989), any additional major project opportunities might have put a strain on capacity levels and thus operating capability and skills constraints became a key factor as well as financial constraint in pursuing opportunity joint ventures.
- For IDV, the main issue highlighted is one of prioritisation of disparate kinds of investment including acquisitive brand development and also organic and acquisitive channel development, together with operational investment. This prioritisation was made more difficult because of major uncertainties associated with external change.
- For London Underground, the increasing amount of funds devoted to safety expenditure appeared to be in tension with the need to invest in improving standards of passenger comfort. Yet managers saw the latter as being imperative in order to catch up with the pressure of external change and public expectations.
- Finally, for Post Office Counters, the pressure of external change to keep pace with client and customer expectations produced a perceived imbalance between the demand for improvement of the network of offices and availability of resource. This may have inhibited projects involving a high degree of innovation and perceived risk.

In conclusion, the macro-linkages explored above do represent an important first hurdle to be surmounted in order to grasp the appraisal problem as a whole. Again, the reader can perhaps reflect on his own situation by asking the following key questions:

- Does your business have a sufficiently clear 'mission' (or 'strategic intent') from which a 'clear strategic vision' to drive investment appraisal can be derived?
- Does this 'mission' explicitly cover the goal of enhancing shareholder value, and also (where appropriate) suggest any constraints on pursuing that value?
- Does your business strategy provide a sufficiently clear view of intended areas of competitive advantage to drive the micro-level analysis for particular long-term financial decisions?
- To what extent do appraisal difficulties reflect problems in coping with external and internal change and stickiness in reallocating resources as opposed to being purely a 'technical' appraisal problem?

ANALYTICAL AND CONTENT LINKAGES AND TENSIONS

Managers' perspectives in the four cases suggest a number of discrete or micro-level issues. These are addressed as follows:

- Identifying the unit and level of analysis
- Evaluating intangibles
- Evaluating contingent events
- Cost/benefit analysis of business complexity
- Evaluating the base case
- Evaluating terminal value
- Conclusions on micro-linkages.

Identifying the unit and level of analysis

First, the issue of identifying the unit of analysis goes back to the question of how the investment need or opportunity was recognised. If an idea surfaces spontaneously within an organisation, then unless this can be readily compared against a formal or informal picture of the strategy it is likely that the project definition may crystallise in relative isolation (for example, Post Office Counters' innovative projects). This may make justifying the project more difficult as there will be, at best, implicit notions of links to strategy. Also, it will be harder to evaluate synergies with other areas of value creation unless these are very direct and tangible. Where the financial impact of a project may reside in value created indirectly, and where it is difficult to identify discrete cash flow benefits, this may also pose major problems for justifying the project (for example, image-related investment at London Underground).

This suggests that three factors would represent improvements to future management practice generally. First, it would be useful for appraisal teams to have ready access to a view of the organisation's strategic direction, its competitive scope and intended sources of competitive advantage *prior* to evaluating any strategic investment decision. This could enable strategic objectives for projects to be more readily defined and projects to be reshaped via strategic and value-based questioning. Equally valuable would be for teams to have a prior and shared view of the key operational interdependencies within the business to evaluate the *indirect* value created by the project. This might well be complemented by modelling tools combining financial *and* operational analysis of any important market variables, including likely competitor reaction. Third, value may also be usefully segmented, for example to distinguish determinate versus contingent value; value gained by protecting existing business versus value generated by b

generated over medium-term versus longer-ter

market segment and finally, synergistic valu

enable managers in other cases to understan

investment portfolio and individual decisi

segmentation should not, however, be used

bureaucracy but should be applied so as to roc...

collectively on the question of 'how does this financial decision gen...

value for the shareholder?'

Evaluating intangibles

Turning now to the specific issue of intangibles, according to prior theory 'intangibles' appeared to be those residual areas of perceived value which could not be readily and objectively quantified. The four cases highlighted that intangibles are a mixed bag which needs to be disaggregated.

'Intangibles' gives an aura of being 'beyond touch or sight', or being almost ghostly in nature. From the cases, this idea appears linked also to a fear that because they are 'beyond touch or sight' then they may not exist (Rolls Royce and IDV best exemplify this). But if managers cannot touch or see them, then by implication they must sense them by some intuitive means. However, unless we are prepared to imagine some sort of dualism of value – one dimension being tangible and measurable, the other being intangible and ghostly – then evidence that intangible value exists must come indirectly. This data must presumably be derived, therefore, from tangible events whether these are external or internal, present or future. The question remaining is 'how can intangibles be understood sufficiently in order to place some broad value on them?'

The four core cases help us to address this question in the following way:

- Intangibles can be categorised into generic groupings, for example, some with internal focus and some with external focus, some being present and some being future (of a contingent nature).
- Some areas of intangibles are amenable to measurement in terms of their likely impact on the external business environment. Others (as they are future) still may be contingent and therefore can be measured only when and if certain events happen. Depending upon the nature of the intangible, the type of measure applied may differ, but the common feature is that this should hinge either around assumed

...s which might create or destroy value, or around the conditions ...der which it is assumed that these events may occur.

...le 9.3 attempts to categorise these intangibles. In the majority of cases ...hese intangibles are either externally facing or are future orientated (and sometimes both). Where these are outward facing these appear more to be measurable in terms of the criteria of the marketplace. In that sense, value in the hands of the marketplace *is* measurable for these intangibles. But, as value is generated by intangibles for a business only through impact on the key value and cost drivers of the business (some of which are indirect), then internal value cannot therefore be measured exactly and in precise financial terms.

Only in the cases of spin-off opportunity and flexibility in Table 9.3 does *uncertainty* emerge as a major issue – the core issue being one of interdependency. This also suggests a useful distinction between intangibles and uncertainty: intangibles appear to be *areas of value which are difficult to define and to set measures for*, whilst uncertainty is more to do with those factors leading to *a range of measurements of value*. Therefore longer-term financial decisions can involve two sources of difficulty – the first being estimation-related difficulty, and the second where measurement post-implementation is a problem. (The latter problem may arise particularly where the organisation lacks monitoring systems for less tangible areas of value.)

Table 9.3 suggests a hierarchical series of questions for evaluating the value of investment decisions, as below:

1. What is being invested in (ie the level and unit of analysis)?
2. What is the nature of the value being created (tangible, less tangible or intangible)?
3. How are the factors which drive value likely to vary (uncertainty)?
4. How do these factors link together (interdependency)?

This suggests that the worst-case appraisal situation for managers is therefore one where value is *a)* hard to define, *b)* hard to understand, *c)* hard to predict, and *d)* involves highly interdependent assumptions.

Many of the areas for measurement suggested in this table involve specifying the *conditions* under which value is likely to arise rather than its direct manifestation. Again, this does not lead mechanistically to a single, determinate value but to a value which is conditional.

In conclusion, intangibles turn out to be intangible for a variety of reasons. But these have the common theme of being part of *systems of interdependency*, some of which are more predictable and measurable than others. Value appears hard to measure, either because the only way to quantify 'value' is through measurement of a system or interface *external* to the organisation, or because of internal *interdependency*, or because of future *contingency*. As financial appraisal is focused on internal value measurement of a fixed 'unit of analysis' and with (assumed to be) determinate cash flows, it is no wonder that the problem of intangibles causes such headaches for a financial purist.

Table 9.3   Types of intangibles and possible measures

Types of intangibles	Related to other appraisal problems	Possible focus for measurement
Product image	Customer value	Customer views of product
Reduced customer costs and risks	Customer value	Customer views of product and service
Customer loyalty	Customer value	Estimated revenue and likelihood of switching
Protection of existing business	Protective investment, the base case	Monitoring incidence of lost business
Spin-off opportunity	Contingent value and interdependency	Specify conditions under which opportunity arises and is harvested
Flexibility	External and internal interdependency	Specify conditions under which flexibility will add value
Cost savings elsewhere	Internal interdependency	Before and after measurement of cost drivers and of impact
Alignment of external and internal factors	External and internal interdependency	Specification of conditions under which alignment may occur and probable value

Many of the problems associated with intangibles may occur because managers often assume that 'value' must be *a)* measurable, *b)* measurable precisely and *c)* measurable in financial terms. We have seen that in many situations intangibles may *not* be precisely measured – and certainly not in financial terms – but this need not inhibit putting a value on them based on a mix of qualitative and quantitative assumptions. This *does not* preclude measurement of attained benefits – indeed 'the measures' may be principally of an operational or market-based nature rather than financially based.

Evaluating contingent events

The next theme to be examined was that of contingent events which pose special problems on linking strategic to financial appraisal at the micro-level. Examples of these were, for value creating events, the selection of a winning brand idea by IDV, or alternatively, events which threaten value including infrequent events with high negative impact (for example those relating to safety at London Underground and security at Post Office Counters).

Managers may find it difficult to value contingent events simply because they are relatively unlikely. Unless the probability of a positive outcome exceeds a particular threshold then it may be very hard for managers to feel confident enough to include this in the value of any investment case. Leaving aside for the moment important questions of setting control measures, there may also be difficulties for managers in including contingent value within an investment case where there is a *major chance* that it will not materialise.

An interesting question would be at what cut-off point this is likely to happen (at a 75 per cent, 50 per cent, or a 25 per cent probability?). Also, how variable is this between individual managers, teams of managers between organisations and also between types and contexts of decisions? Unfortunately the four cases alone are insufficient from which to draw any definitive answer to this question. Managers may well find it difficult to justify including a quantified value for a contingent event unless the balance of probabilities was *at least* in its favour. (One might speculate that this level of probability may be, say, over 50 or even 75 per cent, depending upon how managers apply control measures).

There may also be a further cut-off point, at which level of perceived probability a contingent event is deemed to be worthwhile, including within any *qualitative* assessment of value (that is as an upside to the business case). Again, the cases indicate that managers may feel uncomfortable in incorporating unquantified value as positive 'add-ons' to the investment case. One helpful idea was generated by the Rolls Royce case of distinguishing phases in the creation of demand when:

- demand is *conceivable* – it is relatively indeterminate as buyers may not have defined intent to buy something at all, nor what their specific needs might be;

- demand is *contingent* – buyers are becoming clearer that they will have a need that will require satisfaction but that they are unclear how best to meet that need;
- demand has *crystallised* – buyers have made a clear commitment to a course of action, either through explicit decision or through establishing a predictable pattern of buying.

Estimating the value of opportunities which are based on *conceivable* demand would therefore appear to be best addressed by broad-brush thinking. This might involve exploring the overall shape and size of market demand and potential advantage of the product, given some view of competitor intent and insight into likely customer requirement. Where demand is *contingent* then a more firm estimate of demand might be assessable through more in-depth market analysis as the shape of demand firms up.

Where, however, demand is contingent or conceivable, there may be severe boundaries to the use of financial appraisal tools. This is, perhaps, the territory of the 'unknowable'. In this case, managers may find the use of techniques such as NPV to have a 'fraudulent feel' – unless of course they are aware that the deductive rules for prioritisation (as per financial theory) may not be valid and that measures, for example of NPV, are *illustrative* only. NPV would still be useful as a tool here as it would be possible to work backwards to explore the kind of market conditions in which a positive NPV would appear viable (rather than using market and operational assumptions to generate the NPV).

Cost/benefit analysis of business complexity

This is an area where strategic and financial appraisal can be complementary, and may occur when evaluating the effect of adding incremental activity to an existing business. It may be easy to fall into the trap of thinking that the incremental costs are purely those which are measurable. But in practice, by adding progressively to complexity of activities this may result in additional costs illustrated in the curve in Figure 9.5.

In Figure 9.5 the beneficial effects of economies of scale are increasingly negated by the effect of distraction. This is caused by a loss of focus as complexity increases. For instance, this may be a factor at work in IDV's problem of being able to manage a large range of products and variants through distribution channels and (potentially) in Rolls Royce in covering as broad a range as possible. But the problem arises when

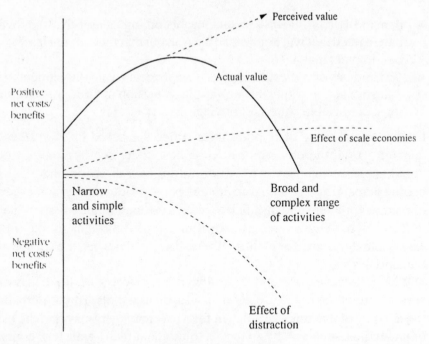

Figure 9.5 Schematic analysis of cost/benefits of narrow versus broad
and complex activities

managers evaluate incremental benefits through assessing, for example,
scale economies but ignore the incremental distraction costs.

Evaluating the base case

Turning to the *base case*, financial theory provides few clues on how to
construct cash flows other than through extrapolation from past, internal
trends. But extrapolated projections may not pick up external trends,
especially those associated with a declining competitive position, and will
almost certainly omit discontinuities.

However, strategic analysis might enable the effects of changes in
competitive position achieved through making particular investment
decisions to be incorporated into the analysis. For instance, there may be
a base level of investment required simply to maintain the level of service
required by customers with changing expectations (London Underground passengers, for example, also travel on British Rail). Also, there
might be an additional amount of investment required to shift relative
perception of that service. Finally, it may require understanding of the
external market to establish whether this relative improvement requires

to be of a certain quantum level to generate sufficient value to trigger an increase in volume or to support a sustainable price rise.

The above examples suggest that the base case cannot be defined simply through extrapolation of steady state conditions nor by projecting the existing rate of decline. Instead, this requires thinking through the dynamic conditions of change in the market place and in change in positioning over time. It also demands an understanding of how improvements may impact on customer satisfaction, on value creation, on value capture and therefore on financial performance. Underlying relationships between value and investment may thus be sticky; they may involve step changes rather than be straightforward linear relationships.

Evaluating terminal value

Finally, *terminal value* poses difficulties of prediction towards the end of the time horizon of foreseeability. If the terminal value is struck at the cut-off point where foreseeability ends then it may appear contradictory to try to build a scenario at that point in time. However, if the main features within that scenario are capable of being pictured, then highlighting this as an overall view may provide a *test of consistency* for whether the terminal value makes sense or not.

Conclusions – analytical and content linkages and tensions

To conclude this subsection on analysis linkages our findings are:

- The decisions which are most difficult to appraise are typically those which are inherently hard to define, hard to understand (due to 'value' being a mixture of things), hard to predict, and involving highly interdependent assumptions.
- Definition of the 'unit of analysis' can be helped by understanding the strategic objectives of the project and in proactive searching for alternative options.
- Different investment decisions may generate value in quite varying ways – it may be thus helpful to segment the ways in which value is being treated, not only to understand the corporate portfolio of business investments but also individual longer-term financial decisions.
- The issue of defining the unit of analysis suggested the benefit of having a picture of the 'strategy' precommunicated to key decision-takers and their advisers. This can be used as a basis for not only

assessing 'strategic fit' of a project, but also the setting of specific strategic objectives aimed at adding value to the competitive strategy.

- *Intangibles* were revealed to be measurable by a variety of ways (often non-financial and external or operational) from which financial value could be inferred, but where value is not created mechanistically. Measures might be set by specifying the conditions under which value might be created rather than specifying exact value. Finally, the *cost/benefits of complexity* may depend on a number of factors driving value, which may interact in non-linear ways.

- Contingent value poses special problems partly as managers have cognitive limitations in evaluating subjective probabilities which conspire with concerns about how control and rewards systems may or may not bite. A helpful distinction may be to analyse uncertain market demand by categorising this as either *conceivable, contingent* or *crystallised*. This may encourage more creative thinking about how to value future opportunity which is affected by compounding uncertainty. But this evaluation is likely to be inhibited by the perceived need to set *controls* for value and also to avoid loss of credibility in business costs. In addition, there are likely to be difficulties in incorporating 'softer value' due to the difficulty of changing control and rewards systems, and also inertia of existing appraisal style. This may well entail extension of and refocusing of measurement systems to track operational and market-related variables, deemphasising financial measures to some extent.

- The base case reveals that there may be complex factors at work in shaping the erosion of value in the 'without-investment case'. This involves the assessment of quantum leaps in performance to trigger perceived customer value, understanding the conditions under which that value is then captured, and identifying how these behave as step changes rather than as simpler, linear relationships.

- Finally, the terminal value of an investment may be usefully underpinned by creating a broad view of the scenario. This provides a 'consistency check' on assumptions about states of the world beyond the zone of the 'readily foreseeable'.

In summary, relatively few inherent tensions of an *analytical* nature are apparent in the fit of strategic and financial appraisal tools. The tensions which existed appeared to revolve around issues such as:

1. the use of payback to set artificially high financial hurdles to encourage targeting behaviour;
2. the fear that investment projects with positive NPV might dilute

reported earnings and thereby provoke a negative response from external capital markets;
3. concern that including 'softer' areas of value would open up the way for manipulation of what would otherwise be 'hard' numbers; and
4. problems of control and measurement subsequent to implementation.

These issues, however, appear to concern organisational behaviour (to which we now turn) rather than problems of a fundamentally conceptual nature.

DECISION PROCESS AND ORGANISATIONAL LEARNING

Key factors affecting the linkage problem

Turning next to the key factors in the management *process* affecting the linkage of strategic and financial appraisal, the following pattern of enablers and constraints emerges.

Enabling factors

- The availability of DCF tools potentially (but not necessarily) provides a vehicle for trading off short- and long-term time horizons in managers' thinking. Despite the criticisms by the 'anti-numbers school' of the use of financial appraisal techniques described in Chapter 4 of this book, without DCF to assist in the decision-making basis, managers might adopt an even shorter-term focus than they would otherwise.
- Developing planning processes with a longer-term and externally orientated approach may pave the way for managers to begin thinking about longer-term financial decisions in a more strategic and less isolated and tactical sense.
- The definition of a corporate or business mission or 'strategic intent' may also enable projects to have clearer strategic objectives.
- The process for planning an investment programme may be best begun by communicating overall strategic objectives from the business plan. This may also help managers to define longer-term financial decisions according to how these add value to the strategy, rather than working primarily on a 'bottom-up' basis on individual decisions. This process might also encourage managers to see project definition more as fluid rather than as fixed, for example by reformulating proposals to add more value with lower cost and risk, and by reviewing strategic alternatives.

Constraining factors

Factors which appeared to constrain the linkage between strategic and financial appraisal in the decision process included:

- incrementalism in the decision-making process;
- fragmentation in decision systems;
- selectiveness in defining 'investment' as primarily 'capital';
- focus on easy-to-quantify value;
- discomfort on the need for subjective judgement.

First, dealing with the problem of decision-making in 'increments'. Decision-making which is in 'incremental' mode, both strategically and financially, may also be reinforced by operational incrementalism. This involves looking at operational needs in a narrow way and ignoring or down-playing interdependencies when framing longer-term financial decisions. The advantages of taking a more holistic view of the decision in context were highlighted in the cases (eg by Rolls Royce and London Underground). A particularly useful idea was that of evaluating a group of decisions or projects as a 'strategic project set', rather than in isolation.

Second, decision and control systems dealing with longer-term financial decisions may be multiple and complex. Longer-term financial decisions might be appraised through capital investment cases, through acquisition cases, or through revenue budgets (for example IDV's brands). These decisions were also reflected, in varying degrees, in strategic and shorter-term business plans. The range of decision systems involved means that managers need to work very hard at achieving an overall vision, especially where planning processes have a bias primarily towards operational and financial analysis.

Third, many longer-term financial decisions which have the fundamental characteristics of longer-term investment may not be evaluated as such (eg brands at IDV; corporate image at Post Office Counters). Where investment is measured as a 'revenue cost' (and thus not capitalised nor subject to a project management process) it is easy for managers not to realise that it involves cash flows of an 'investment' nature. For example, a major restructuring or reorganisation may be, in effect, a long-term investment. Another example might be a joint venture which may require commitment to cash flows which, even though they might not involve a major up-front investment, may involve considerable lags before returns are recouped.

Fourth, linkages may also be constrained by concerns that incorporating 'softer' areas of value (contingent value, opportunity value on intangibles) might undermine the credibility of investment cases. It would also undermine control processes as currently configured in many, if not most, companies.

Fifth, managers involved in the four core cases also appeared to be uncomfortable with the degree to which they needed to rely on subjective judgement to make decisions. In one case this appeared to be compounded by a fear of finding out just how uncertain the key assumptions underlying a strategic investment decision were. Yet subjective judgement may have a vitally important role to play in bringing together an overall view of the decision, in reconciling 'hard' and 'soft' indicators of value, and in drawing on past experience, both within the company and from other organisational environments.

SUMMARY AND CONCLUSIONS

Our conclusions on the problems of linking strategic and financial appraisal can now be summarised.

A major reason why managers have problems in linking strategic and financial appraisal is because there are just so many areas of potential linkage. These individual linkages are also complex, and are typically of a qualitative or semi-quantitative nature. Any idea of creating a simple and single analytical framework for linking strategic and financial appraisal across a diversity of investment decisions therefore appears to be a task doomed to failure.

However, there *are* a number of areas where linkages between strategic and financial appraisal might be fruitfully created. These include understanding the relationships at the macro- (or process) level between mission, strategy and value. They also include understanding relationships between strategy, change and investment mix. In addition, there are analytical linkages and areas of potential tension in defining the level and unit of analysis, and how to deal with intangibles and contingent value, evaluating the cost/benefits of business complexity, the base case and terminal value.

Whilst there are common patterns in problems across diverse organisations, variations in the business context for investment decisions are considerable. The key variables here are the varying timescales over which financial decisions are made, the underlying degree of uncertainty, their mutual interdependency and also the past experience base of individuals, appraisal teams and the organisation generally. These variations need to be tackled by managers on a case-by-case basis and involve managers unravelling what may appear to be a 'unique' set of problems by use of generic approaches and methods. This implies that a simplistic and prescriptive approach to dealing with the problem of linking strategic and financial is inappropriate. Rather managers might better adopt a semi-structured, *questioning* approach.

Besides the *analytical* problem of linking strategic and financial appraisal is also a perhaps more difficult, behavioural and organisational one of introducing change in strategic and financial decision systems. As Chapter 8 on BP highlighted, to do a 'thorough job' requires a change in routines and thinking led from the very top and sustained over a number of years.

A series of semi-structured questions which can be used as checklists for decision-making is contained in Appendix I which is a key part of this book. Besides linking directly to the findings of this chapter, they have been additionally refined through advisory work in a number of companies. They are thus presented in a form which can be readily tailored to your own business needs.

10

CONCLUSIONS

KEY LESSONS FOR THEORY AND PRACTICE

This book began by highlighting some consequences of longer-term financial decision-making which appeared to have gone wrong. It then suggested that the lack of clear linkage between strategic and financial theory might be a major contributory factor in this process. Following this, it was argued that financial theory provides only a part of the effective 'treatment' for these problems. The problems which appeared to be most intractable when applying financial tools appeared to be precisely those where strategic appraisal could play a role, such as intangibles, uncertainty, interdependency and the value of contingent opportunities.

Traditional strategic theory rooted in corporate planning on its own did not appear to provide 'the answer' to this problem. Corporate planning approaches on their own appeared to be too broad to provide managers with the concrete and detailed guidance required for specific decisions. But by forging closer linkages between strategic and financial theory it has been shown by the Cranfield cases that managers *can* achieve some valuable insights into how to deal with these issues. Strategic analysis appears to have provided help to research participants in understanding what is being invested in and why, and how individual decisions relate to other areas of business investment and operational change. Financial analysis also showed the potential of being able to focus strategic thinking, for example in capturing trade-offs in evaluating major longer-term financial decisions (at Rolls Royce), and also in the BP case in Chapter 8. Strategic and financial appraisal can thus provide complementary views on longer-term financial decisions – whilst strategy can provide the broader *vision*, finance can provide greater *precision*.

What was also highlighted was that these hard-won insights on linkages require a large and sustained effort to transform decision-making processes. This may require a programme of change and organisational learning involving the likely adaptation of planning, control and rewards systems (again, the BP case highlighting the amount of effort required).

Although the transition towards closer linkages of strategic and financial thinking may take a long time for a particular organisation, it may take us even longer to shift patterns of thinking in the academic, management and professional environment. Generations of managers and accountants have been groomed in thinking that longer-term financial decisions involve merely technically-based *investment appraisal* which equates more or less with *financial appraisal* and also with *capital project appraisal.* Strategy may also be seen as inquiring about more remote issues such as 'business direction' which they do not relate quickly and easily to in the making of longer-term financial decisions. The scale of the reorientation process involved to effect this transition facing us is therefore daunting.

The lessons for practice can perhaps now be best summarised in the following ten points:

1. The definition of any specific, longer-term financial decision is one which should be fluid and, if necessary, iterated.
2. The decision should be viewed in context to understand its fit with mission, its strategic objectives, its operational linkages and the appropriateness of its timing and management's commitment to make it succeed.
3. Analysis should be pre-focused on a balance of key internal *and external* assumptions. External analysis should expose key uncertainties to explore the full impact (both present and future) on the value of the decision.
4. The 'do nothing' or base case does not mean that 'nothing happens': the base case may well involve an insidious decline which should be explicitly addressed in the business case and benchmarked.
5. Less tangible benefits and costs *must* be explored whether these are formally included in the financial appraisal or not.
6. Wherever possible, less tangible benefits should be financially quantified, even if this is to be achieved in broad terms, so that prioritisation of various decisions is evenly balanced and so that feedback on less tangible value is provided to management. If this is not feasible, market or operational measures ought to be possible surrogates.
7. Operational analysis should also be used to creatively reshape the project and should highlight any aspects where the project takes the organisation beyond its core experience base and competencies.

8. Subjective judgement should not be used as a substitute for analysis but as an essential element in balancing views of an opportunity. In their management process, managers need to evolve ways of sharing and testing judgements to avoid the appraisal process becoming purely bureaucratic.
9. The appraisal process is one which involves complex learning. The learning outputs should be capitalised on in an effective way and should not be lost through a witch-hunting, post-audit process.
10. Managers need to become more skilled in the process of 'managing uncertainty'. They need to surface and understand areas of uncertainty and anxiety even when this becomes extreme and fear-provoking. These high impact/high uncertainty areas need to be monitored rather than put aside.

NEXT STEPS

If this book has succeeded in enthusing the reader to improve decision-making (and thus involving change), at the same time he might be daunted by the prospect of beginning on the road to implementation. In order to get started on this process the following suggestions may prove useful:

- A digestible area of experimentation is identified (eg a particular business unit or a major project). Alternatively (as in the BP example), it is possible to begin by comparing estimates of NPV of projected post-tax cash flows of strategic business units and corporate head office with the stock market value of the group.
- Any pilot should be targeted at procuring some early, tangible benefits (for example, insights in an area which has previously been highly ambiguous or contentious).
- Following experimentation, a 'first-cut' revised framework for appraisal can then be distilled (perhaps using the checklist of questions in Appendix I as a starting point).
- Further to application across a range of decision areas and businesses, a short 'learning review' of the value which has been added by the revised appraisal framework should be conducted. It is suggested that this is best conducted in a workshop environment to amplify and encapsulate learning.
- The related areas of organisational decision, control and rewards systems also impacted by these changes should then be addressed to make consistent with the framework, for example revenue budgets.

But most important of all is that these changes need to be progressively owned and internalised by key stakeholders. These include those championing new strategic opportunity through to those making an independent review of business cases, at business and corporate levels.

If my book has triggered in its readers an eagerness to drive strategic and financial appraisal of longer-term financial decisions much closer together, then it will certainly have achieved its ambitions.

CHECKLIST FOR APPRAISAL OF LONGER-TERM FINANCIAL DECISIONS

This checklist is intended as a foundation for managers who may, having read this book, now seek to tailor their appraisal approaches. This is structured to take you through each phase of the appraisal process in the following stages:

- Defining the financial decision
- Analysis of external assumptions
- Analysis of internal assumptions
- Defining the base case
- Exploring interdependencies
- Evaluating intangibles
- Evaluating the overall business case
- Feedback via learning, control and rewards systems.

This checklist can be applied with appropriate tailoring where necessary to the following areas:

Acquisitions
Brand investment
Capital plant and equipment
Change programmes
Corporate re-organisation
Diversification options
Image development
Information and communications technology and systems
Joint ventures and collaborative deals
Large-scale construction projects
Market penetration

Product development
Reappraisal of an existing strategic business unit
Research and development
Shareholder value appraisal of a corporate portfolio
Technology acquisition
Training and management development expenditure

I. Defining the financial decision

1. What are the key strategic objectives of the financial decision?
2. What is the precise scope of the decision (present and future)?
3. How does it link to other new projects and to existing business activities?
4. Should it be evaluated, not on a 'stand-alone' basis, but as part of a set of projects or decisions?
5. Should it be disaggregated into a number of sub-projects or decisions?
6. What (genuine) alternatives may exist to the specific proposal in meeting its overall strategic objectives?
7. Does the project definition explicitly seek to build in an element of flexibility to reduce risk should the internal or external environment change?

II. Analysis of external assumptions

1. How does the value of the opportunity depend on the company's external environment (directly or indirectly)?
2. Where the opportunity depends upon market demand, what competitive assumptions are assumed upon which volumes, prices and margins are based?
3. Why is the assumed *competitive position* believed to be sustainable during the middle and latter part of the life cycle of the opportunity?
4. What new competitive conditions may occur, and how might these impact on the value of the opportunity (eg substitutes, new entrants, industry restructuring)?
5. More particularly, how might specific competitors be either addressing the same opportunity already or be able to respond quickly?
6. How do customers perceive the relative value of any end product or service upon which the opportunity depends? (Consider perceived image, cost savings, risk levels).
7. How powerful are customers relative to the company and to what

extent is the additional value created harvested by customers versus the company?

8. What life cycle characteristics does the market opportunity depend upon (product or technology life cycles, industry life cycles, economic life cycles)?

9. How might these life cycles effect impact, not merely the quantity of demand but also its quality? What might shorten the life cycle of the opportunity?

10. What other regulatory factors might impact on the value of the opportunity?

11. If the value of the opportunity is dependent upon market growth, what are the factors which will sustain growth and under what circumstances may these cease to operate, and with what effect?

12. Have the growth rate and the projections of margins taken into account individual assumptions for each segment of the market, each distribution channel, and each major type of customer etc?

13. What underlying market shares are assumed and on what basis have these 'markets' been defined?

14. What key trends may cause customer demand to shift over the period of the opportunity?

III. Analysis of internal assumptions

1. What are the likely effects on reducing unit cost through gaining assumed economies of scale? Also, to what extent are unit costs increased if volumes are significantly less than 'most likely' assumptions?

2. What capacity levels are assumed and are these assessed in relation to the operating cycle over a whole annual period?

3. Are unit costs likely to increase considerably as output reaches near capacity levels?

4. What other unforeseen areas of investment may be required either of a future or indirect nature (eg expansion of office space) not currently included in 'incremental' cash flows?

5. How have 'incremental costs' been defined and in particular how do cost apportionments incorporate a 'fair' allowance for direct and indirect resources absorbed by the activity?

6. What further technical breakthroughs are assumed in order to support assumed levels of productivity?

7. Are timescales for implementation, and in particular learning to use

new methods in practice, realistic (for instance, to achieve required quality levels)?

8. Are there adequate operational resources to implement the project especially where this relies upon scarce management and technical skills?

9. Is the area of opportunity one where the organisation (and key individuals) has both the capability, the commitment and, where relevant, the appropriate culture to make it a success?

IV. Defining the base case

1. Where the 'base case' assumes improving external conditions, upon what key competitive assumptions is this based? How may these change?

2. Where the 'base case' suggests the business is in decline, then what are the key competitive assumptions upon which this is based?

3. In a 'declining base case', what could be done to reduce or halt the decline without requiring new investment (eg improvement via operational change)?

4. What degree of uncertainty surrounds the pace of decline of the 'base case'?

5. Where the 'base case' for the business unit overall is difficult to define or predict, what is the approximate value of a 'protective' nature which managers put on the decision's defensive benefits?

6. Does the degree of decline of the base case suggest that the business unit overall should be fundamentally reappraised?

V. Exploring interdependencies

1. What are the key interdependencies between external assumptions (eg between regulatory change and market growth and structure; between economic slowdown and competitive rivalry, etc)?

2. What are the key interdependencies between internal assumptions (eg between sales of one product cannibalising sales of another product, and between sales of a new product 'piggy-backing' off an existing product)?

3. What are the key interdependencies between external and internal assumptions (eg between assumed intensity of competitive rivalry and price discounting, between perceptions of company image and actual service quality, etc)?

4. What key policy interdependencies exist (eg with corporate intent)

and how may the intent of specific internal and external stakeholders be shaped?

VI. Evaluating intangibles

1. Does much of the value of the opportunity depend on less tangible factors?
2. If so, are these factors measurable at some future point in time in financial terms, or not?
3. Where these are difficult to quantify financially even at some future date, are there other ways of quantifying or assessing whether the benefits have been realised (eg in market-based or operational measures)?
4. If so, is there an 'appropriate worth' that managers would be prepared to pay for these (or alternatively, if they had them, what would they pay to retain them – ie what is their 'deprival value')?
5. Are these benefits difficult to evaluate because they are, in effect, consumed externally (eg by customers)? If so, are these capable of being harvested by extra prices or by avoiding price reduction or avoiding a loss of volume which might otherwise occur?
6. Have all areas of less tangible *costs* been included in the appraisal (for example, does going ahead with the project result in difficult-to-quantify distraction costs as the business becomes increasingly complex)?
7. Where no formal value is put on intangibles, how is it proposed to reflect this value in the decision process, especially where there are tight financial constraints in place?
8. How will less tangible factors be subsequently measured (eg by measuring service levels, customer perceptions, employee perceptions, etc)?
9. Under what specific circumstances will assumed 'synergies' be harvested and how can this be measured?
10. Has future and 'contingent' opportunity which may spin-off from the project been included and, if so, how?
11. Also, might the project foreclose other opportunities of significant value and what is therefore the contingent value *lost* by the opportunity?

VII. Evaluating the overall business case

1. Does the business case specify clearly the scope and objectives of the

investment project, its relationship to other areas of investment (capital or revenue) and to operational change?

2. Does it specify what the strategic routes to value creation are, eg competitive enhancement or protection, versus synergistic value or creating future spin-off opportunities?
3. Are key strategic assumptions clearly identified?
4. Are operational and financial assumptions clearly identified?
5. Are key uncertainties and interdependencies identified?
6. Does the 'sensitivity analysis' focus on key risks and also on exploring worst downsides (and also any 'upsides' which may strain capacity and push up unit cost levels)?
7. Has a break-even analysis been conducted to test the robustness of NPV and does this take each of the high impact, external and internal assumptions in turn?
8. Where the area of opportunity is beyond the past experience base of the management team, how are managers going to avoid major errors and thus an avoidable investment in learning?
9. Have areas of 'softer' value, including intangibles, the protective value from slowing a declining base case, or the value of contingent and future opportunity been identified and, if necessary, isolated in the business case?
10. If the project is targeted at achieving a shorter payback, would this produce some useful reshaping of the 'project definition'?
11. Besides IRR, has NPV also been assessed in order to prioritise projects and has the NPV been compared across projects along with variations in payback? (All other things being equal, a project with faster payback may be preferable to another project with similar NPV.)
12. How does this project affect the total financial balance of the portfolio of projects (or businesses) given its cash flow profile?
13. What is the likely impact on bottom-line earnings? Is this such that the proposal needs to be 'sold' back to the shareholders to highlight longer-term benefits and to shift these perceived constraints?
14. What operational and organisational requirements are required to implement the project satisfactorily?
15. What is the basis for any 'terminal' or residual value which has been included?
16. What strategic questions on 'what business are we in?' has the appraisal raised which need to be addressed in the strategic planning process?
17. Do the 'critical success factors' for successful implementation have

close fit with 'how we do things around here' (paradigm), or is a significant and costly clash likely?

VIII. Feedback via learning, control and rewards systems

1. Is there provision to capture the learning from implementing the opportunity at each major stage?
2. Is it specified *who* this learning will be fed back to in order that the lessons are not buried and that corrective action is triggered?
3. How will controls be operated to monitor internal assumptions beyond the more immediate future?
4. How will controls be used to monitor external change and thus to provide feedback on earlier external assessments?
5. How will controls monitor capture of intangible value without producing a panoply of bureaucracy?
6. How will managers be rewarded and recognised for achievement of projections? Will this take into account 'controllable' versus 'non-controllable' variables?

APPENDIX 2

SUMMARY OF RESEARCH METHODOLOGY

INTRODUCTION

As this book is primarily a guide for the practitioner rather than an academic work, details of the methodology followed are kept brief in this Appendix. Nevertheless it is useful to summarise the research approach both to support the findings and suggestions made to managers in linking corporate strategy, value and investment decisions, and also for the interest of the academic reader.

This summary runs as follows:

- The focus of the research – 'managers' perspectives'
- The qualitative and interpretative nature of the research
- The strategy, structure and style of the learning process
- Qualitative data collection, analysis and interpretation
- Conclusions and implications of methodology

The focus of the research – 'managers' perspectives'

Much strategic management research focuses at the organisational level, with the consequence that the role which individual managers play in the decision process is down-played. Yet it is ultimately managers as individual actors or as small groups who take the key decisions which shape the strategic path of their organisations.

Strategic management issues are highly complex and strain managers' cognitive abilities to the limit – especially when this is looked at in the context of the fragmentary and disjointed decision-making environment where managers operate. These difficulties are compounded when managers are asked to make linkages between corporate strategy, value and investment decisions.

This research's starting point was to seek, therefore, to understand managers' *own understanding* as individuals of the linkage problem, rather than to survey the tools and techniques of appraisal which happened to be in use. This understanding is not a simple, unitary thing but is a set of *perspectives* (Mezirow, 1977)[1] on the problems which require in depth investigation to be properly understood.

The qualitative and interpretative nature of the research

The research therefore departs from past tradition in focusing on surveys of management practice which characterises the bulk of the *empirical* financial literature on the topic. Rather, it seeks an *interpretative* account of managers' perspectives (Burrell and Morgan, 1979)[2] and is therefore more within the tradition of researchers who are at the boundary between strategic and organisational theory.

The research is exploratory and explanatory, rather than descriptive or seeking broadly-based generalisations. Also, as the focus of the research was managers' perspectives – cognitive and affective characteristics which are complex and in flux – then a qualitative approach appeared to be the most effective research strategy.

The strategy, structure and style of the learning process

As the research was aimed at revealing managers' perspectives, a vehicle was sought which would flush these perspectives out fully rather than partially. In order to do this it was decided that a *learning process* (Cohen and Manion, 1980)[3] provided the ideal strategy to achieve this. By putting managers in a situation in which they had little choice but to reveal these perspectives, the best chance of surfacing these perspectives in their entirety was secured.

The research structure was therefore to begin that collection with a series of non-directive interviews which were audiotaped. These interviews were held in-company. Next, two managers from the four separate organisations came together in a two and a half day workshop to share issues and approaches, and also to reflect on learning inputs which were derived from a framework of 'current knowledge on the linkages'. This framework was structured and presented as a 'non-prescriptive' set of prompts and ideas. As managers had already been interviewed and much of their preexisting perspectives surfaced and analysed, it was then possible to detect changes in perspectives of which a number occurred. This first workshop was followed by a debriefing interview thus enabling a fix on the 'after' state of perspectives to be determined. All interactions during this (and the succeeding workshop) were video recorded enabling any input to be revisited in terms of content and context.

After the debriefing interviews, a period of six months then followed during which managers were able to experiment with any new insights, to implement any action plans or investigate approaches in contact with other companies both within and outside the research consortium. The learning outputs of the process were then recorded through a further review workshop where, following individual presentations, managers again debated the issues to establish where they had made progress in achieving greater clarity , where they had not and, if not, why not.

The research process thus involved triangulation of data from a number of sources, including:

- Interviews versus workshops
- Between managers from the same company
- Pre-, post- and during the learning process.

Qualitative data collection, analysis and interpretation

The research vehicle yielded a mountain of qualitative data which was transcribed manually. A grounded approach (Glaser and Strauss, 1967[4]; Strauss, 1987[5]) was used to look for naturally suggested categories of perspectives and to interpret patterns in the data and evolve theory generation. The output was fed back to managers in the form of 'case histories' which were subsequently distilled into Chapters 6 and 7 of this book. This was an invaluable check on the researcher's own interpretations.

Besides this grounded approach (which was found indispensable given the richness and complexity of data), mapping approaches to strategic thinking were also used (Huff, 1990[6]), especially in the theory-building stage and for comparative analysis between cases to establish how the multitude of issues interacted in managers' own perspectives.

Conclusions and implications of methodology

Although proving hard to implement, the methodology proved highly effective in surfacing and exploring managers' perspectives on this complex problem. This suggests that the combination of qualitative methodology, a learning process and mapping of patterns in strategic thought may prove a powerful combination for exploring other strategic management issues.

REFERENCES

1. Mezirow, J (1977) 'Perspective Transformation' in *Studies in Adult Education*, 9, no. 2, NIAE, Leicester, pp 159–169
2. Burrell, B and Morgan, G (1979) *Sociological Paradigms and Organisational Analysis*, Heinemann, London
3. Cohen, L and Manion, L (1980) *Research Methods in Education*, Croom Helm Ltd, Beckenham
4. Glaser, B G and Strauss, A L (1967) *The Discovery of Grounded Theory*, Aldine, Chicago
5. Strauss, A L (1987) *Qualitative Analysis for Social Scientists*, Cambridge University Press
6. Huff, A S, ed. (1990) *Mapping Strategic Thought*, John Wiley and Sons, Chichester

DETAILED PROCEDURE FOR DISCOUNTING

The procedure for discounting future cash flows involves adjustment of future cash flows to reflect the fact that cash at some future date is worth less than cash held at present. This idea is akin to that of investing in a building society with the expectation that at some future date you will receive *more* money back in the way of principal plus interest, for instance at an interest rate of ten per cent. Discounting is, in effect, the same procedure in reverse – the investor would be indifferent between having, for instance, £121 after two years and £100 now, or:

$$\frac{£121}{(1.10) \times (1.10)} \quad = \quad £100$$

where 1·10 is equivalent to one hundred plus ten per cent.

Confusion is most likely to arise when managers are obliged to apply a *discount factor*, whether this is from a discount table or a spreadsheet package. At the end of year 2, one divided by (1.10 times 1.10) is 0.826. The manager may be inclined to ask 'what does this factor of 0.826 mean?' What this means is, given the attitude of the investor to holding money now versus the future, in order to get an equivalent valuation of a cash stream occurring over a period in time he needs to adjust for these (time) preferences.

But the end product of this calculation – the 'present value' – has a 'notional' or 'unreal' feel to it, as the business will never receive in hard cash terms the exact value of the 'present value'. The 'present value' is a mixture of cash flows evaluation using successively harsher discount factors at different points in time.

Nevertheless it *is* possible to revisit a business case by comparing the estimated versus the realised cash flows. The net difference can then be reevaluated by discounting the difference between estimated and realised cash flows. But why is it that audit of post investment cash flows and evaluation of estimated versus realised NPV is like hunting for a rare, if not extinct, species? There appear to be a number of hurdles here, such as managers' fear of revealing that estimates were 'way out'. Also if managers have problems in discounting *future* cash flows – and in understanding what that means – then post cash flows will present even bigger headaches. In addition, there is the concern that this is 'shutting the gate after the horse has bolted'.

This issue is examined closer during the four core cases in Chapters 6 and 7.

It is also easy for managers to fall into a number of other traps in understanding and applying discounting techniques, especially in the following areas:

- Getting confused between the discount rate and, for instance, the rate of return required to compensate for inflation (the discount rate compensates investors for inflation *plus* a real reward for deferring cash into the future *plus* a further premium for risk on that kind of business investment).

- Projecting cash flows in terms which *do not* incorporate expectations of inflation, and then applying an *inflation-included* discount rate to find a present value. The result is then a present value of future cash flows which is artificially low. The rate applied needs to be consistent at all times.

- Deciding that it is just 'all too much' and that payback is an easier way out (but this may produce misleading project comparisons where cash flows are significantly longer than the payback period and vary in both duration and magnitude beyond that period).

Also the *consequences* of applying discounting procedures include, first, that cash inflows later on are, in effect, penalised in the valuation relative to the present value of initial outlays and earlier cash inflows. The higher the discount rate, the more pronounced this penalising and compounding effect will become. This lowers the value of the investment (its net present value, or 'NPV'). If in doubt, look at your discount tables and see the discount factor becoming very small after years six or seven – and disproportionately so when the discount rate exceeds fifteen per cent. At ten years into the future, a ten per cent discount rate gives a discount factor of approximately 0.38, whilst a fifteen per cent discount rate gives a factor of only 0.25.

Second, the assumed 'terminal value' of the investment can play a major role in determining NPV unless it is *a)* included a very long way out into the future; *b)* the investment's capital value is much reduced at the end of its life cycle; *c)* the discount rate is very high or *d)* a mixture of a, b and c occurs. This means that it is easy to manipulate NPV by forming optimistic assumptions for terminal value – a point many readers will no doubt recognise. For example, in one acquisition example which I was involved in, the NPV of the deal doubled if the 'terminal value' was evaluated on a price earning ratio of 15 as opposed to ten.

SUBJECT AND AUTHOR INDEX